T0325293

INDUSTRIAL STRUCTURE
AND ECONOMIC GROWTH

www.royalcollins.com

INDUSTRIAL STRUCTURE
AND ECONOMIC GROWTH

A Refutation of Clark's Law

Ruyu Zhao

Books Beyond Boundaries

ROYAL COLLINS

Industrial Structure and Economic Growth: A Refutation of Clark's Law

Ruyu Zhao

First published in 2022 by Royal Collins Publishing Group Inc.
Groupe Publication Royal Collins Inc.
BKM Royalcollins Publishers Private Limited

Headquarters: 550-555 boul. René-Lévesque O Montréal (Québec) H2Z1B1 Canada
India office: 805 Hemkunt House, 8th Floor, Rajendra Place, New Delhi 110 008

ISBN: 978-1-4878-0964-5

To find out more about our publications, please visit www.royalcollins.com.

Foreword

The emergence and development of science is a constant journey in the development process of knowing more about the world. The simple induction method was first used to sum up the principles of everything. However, new phenomena emerged endlessly. With the expansion of fields of learning and improvements in observation, it was not difficult to find that established theories cannot explain all the facts. Theories became so weak that logical positivism had to treat so-called scientific theories as high-probability events. However, theories that can only explain high-probability events are not scientific at all. Phenomena beyond the scope of interpretation, if any, are sufficient to prove the limitations of the original induction method. For instance, when a "white crow" is discovered, you should realize, in a scientific sense, that the conclusion "all crows under the sun are black" is wrong.

Of course, science is not theology. A science is merely a hypothesis encapsulated by predecessors through induction and logical positivism; it can never touch the ultimate essence of things and can be falsified continuously. Each scientific paradigm only summarizes the characteristics of similar things at a certain level and perspective. The addition of new levels, new perspectives and new cases requires induction at a deeper level closer to the essence.

Therefore, science gradually develops by replacing the old paradigm with a new one; and only the paradigm that enables such replacement is science. For example, cosmology changed from a geocentric model to a heliocentric model, and further extended to the solar system, the galactic system, and the universe ... Every new discovery provides us with a little bit of supplementary information, but this is far from the whole picture. It is through constant falsification that cosmology becomes science.

There is no doubt that scientific progress lies in self-falsification, or more specifically, self-denial of theoretical paradigms. Economics has established itself as a science. However, too many theories have been confronted with contradictions beyond the scope of self-explanation, such as Giffen goods in the market mechanism, Heckscher-Ohlin theory, and Leontief's paradox ... With the passing of time, the "white crow" will continue to come into view.

The theoretical paradigm proposed in this book is a rebuttal of traditional industrial structure theories, represented by Clark's Law. Clark's theoretical paradigm was introduced in the late 19th century and supported by many prominent figures. Among them, several Nobel Prize winners have proved the existence of Clark's Law through their own studies – Kuznets, Chenery, and Bell. However, as they focused on periods between the 1960s and 70s, their insight was blinded by historical limitations. In reality, from the First Industrial Revolution to the present, changes in industrial structure are by no means a one-off process.

The cruel reality is to question the academic conscience of economists – should we adapt economic activity to theory, or bring theory closer to reality? Should we strive for economic prosperity, or yield to economic recession just because it accompanies a high share of services? Should economics seek to maximize benefits under the rational allocation of resources, or follow the existing so-called law and give up the pursuit of prosperity?

Based on the above, the author has realized the limitations of Clark's Law since 1992, and began a journey of exploration whilst undertaking an economics PhD. In 1994, when studying in Japan, he captured a vivid "white crow" for theoretical research from the Japanese economic depression after the collapse of the bubble economy. In December 1996, the author completed his doctoral dissertation, titled "Industrial Structure: Theory and Practice." The *Paradox of the Post-Industrial Society* published in 1999 gave a preliminary summary of the new theoretical paradigm of industrial structure. Since then, research has gone deeper: in 2008, during a visit to Harvard University as a senior visiting scholar of the Ministry of Education, the author further summarized the relationship between industrial structure and economic growth in the United States and in China. The progress of theoretical falsifications constitutes the innovative content of this book.

Looking back at global economic history, there are many examples of long-term depression caused by upsurges in the service sector without the support of the industrial sector. Bitter and far-reaching lessons from the last thirty years include the collapse of Japan's bubble economy, the East Asian financial crisis, and the US subprime mortgage crisis. They have repeatedly falsified Clark's Law. In spite of this, some countries still believe in traditional economic theories and adhere to it. They are infatuated with increasing the share of the service sector; such erroneous thinking can seriously misled economic development at the strategic level. For this reason, we hope that this book can provide implications and inspire reflections for those with the opportunity to change things. We are open to discussions. After all, the purpose of this book is to deepen this area of economic theory through falsification.

Contents

CONTENTS

CONTENTS

CHAPTER 1

The Law of Industrial Structure

Theories on industrial structure originated in the mid-17th century. After the introduction of Clark's Law, the basic theoretical paradigm remained almost the same, however, latecomers advocated post-industrialization. This made Clark's Law even more like an iron law, which could not be challenged or questioned.

Section 1   Theoretical Origin of Clark's Law

Theories on industrial structure go back a long way and have been continuously expanded over time; though considerable progress was only made during the mid-20th century. This chapter presents a brief historical review of Western theories on industrial structure, with William Petty's views used as a starting point – including formation, development and evolution – to illustrate its basic premise and ideas.

I. *William Petty's Inference*

The simplest inference on industrial structure was proposed by William Petty in his work *Political Arithmetick*.[1] Petty was not only the first economist to discuss industrial structure, but also the founding figure of British classical economics. As stated by Karl Marx, Petty integrated views on the source of material wealth into "political arithmetic – political economy in the initial form as an independent science."[2] Furthermore, Petty is regarded as the founder of statistics and econometrics, thanks to its usage in his book.

Political Arithmetick is not devoted to the issue of industrial structure, rather it tries to answer the question of whether Britain can "run the entire business world" through a comparative study of strength among Britain, France, and Holland. In his elaboration, Petty drew special attention to the importance of industry, capital, and income. His inference about industrial structure was drawn during the discussion on "Holland's industrial and commercial interests" in the first chapter, which explores the reasons for strength differences between France and Holland.

Petty argued that, "The revenue of industry is higher than that of agriculture, whereas the revenue of commerce is much higher than that of industry ... Here we have noticed the fact that with the development of industry, commerce and ingenuity, either agriculture will fall back or farmers' wages must be raised, resulting in an inevitable decline in land rent."

Such ideas have their historical origins: from the perspective of economic history, in the pre-industrial stage of the time, commerce was creating prerequisite markets for industry through great geographical discoveries and exploitation. In reality, commerce was in its heyday: Holland indeed established an absolute economic advantage in Europe through its maritime trade. Petty was so misled by this phenomenon that he reversed the internal relationship between the material production sector, especially in industry and commerce – as to which one decides or dominates – leading to strong mercantilist views. However, it should be noted that such views corresponded only to a stage in the evolution of Petty's economic thought, and were completely lost in his later work *Quantulumcunque concerning Money*. As pointed out by Friedrich Engels, "Mercantilist insights contained in his (Petty's) other writings disappeared without trace here."[3]

II.   *Adam Smith's Classical Theory*

Following in Petty's footsteps, Adam Smith also addressed the issue of industrial structure. He lived in the era just before the British Industrial Revolution. At the time, the limitations of mercantilism that hindered industrial progress and the falsehood of prosperity brought about by commerce had been exposed. However, industry was not yet developed and still relied on the support of agriculture. Therefore, Smith's thoughts on industrial structure had a strong physiocratic tendency. Though he did not explicitly propose the concept of industrial structure in *The Wealth of Nations*, Smith discussed industry and its development as well as the order of employing capital.[4]

In the second volume, Smith touched on industrial structure when discussing the "different employments of capitals." The employment of capitals, also known as particular branches of industry, includes i) Procuring the crude produce, i.e., agriculture; ii) Manufacturing and preparing that crude produce, i.e., industry; iii) Transporting the crude or manufactured produce, i.e., wholesale trade, which can be further divided into domestic, foreign, and carrying trade; and iv) Dividing particular portions into smaller parcels, i.e., retail trade.

Regarding the order of employing capital, Smith believed that agriculture comes first and retail comes last: "In agriculture, nature labors along with man." In addition to profit, the rent of land may also be considered as the produce. But exporting the surplus produce to distant markets or exchanging it, for which there is demand, at home enables the division of labor and the development of the market mechanism. Therefore, carrying trade is particularly advantageous to "England whose defense and security depend on water-carriage and boat quantity." For "carrying trade by the value of the surplus produce of all the different countries in the world," its possibilities are "infinite." Therefore, when "prioritizing defense over wealth," Smith recognized the "reward" for sea-carrying trade and the "protection" for particular branches of industry as exceptions to liberalism.

In the third book, Smith stated that, "The great commerce of every civilized society is that carried on between the inhabitants of the town and those of the country. It consists in the exchange of crude for manufactured produce, either immediately, or by the intervention of money, or of some sort of paper which represents money." He then said, "As subsistence is, in the nature of things, prior to conveniency and luxury, so the industry which procures the former, must necessarily be prior to that which ministers to the latter." Smith is referring to this "order," in which growing capital is first directed at agriculture, then manufacturers, and lastly foreign commerce: "This order of things is very natural."

Thus, industry covered by Smith, in short, is agriculture, manufacturing, commerce, and trade (including transportation). The so-called natural order of industry is a model in which investment should be arranged in descending powers of proportion, on condition that the gross national capital is certain. Smith even asserted that without sufficient gross national capital, trade may be necessarily forced into foreign capital. In reality, industry in various countries of Europe, including Britain, basically followed an "unnatural and retrograde order." This is a consequence of the development of industry as the "descendent of trade" prior to the "descendent of agriculture" in modern Europe. Smith said, "In this process, the law of primogeniture and the consequent entails that hinder the division of great landed estates, as well as the domination of merchants and the impact of resulting merchantism cannot be denied." It is clear to see that Smith's economic thought was deeply influenced by "physiocracy," yet compared with Petty's mercantilist thought, it advanced understanding of industrial structure.

III. Fisher's Three-Sector Theory

Industrialization developed by leaps and bounds after the mid-18th century – during the First and Second Industrial Revolutions. With industry development, the service sector also expanded significantly. During the Great Depression in the 1930s, the decline in the industrial sector reflected, statistically, the significant advantage of the service sector. This recalled people to Petty's simple ideas.

New Zealand economist A. G. Fisher brought up Petty's thesis on the basis of statistics and proposed, for the first time, the three-sector classification method in his works *Capital and the Growth of Knowledge* and *Production, Primary, Secondary and Tertiary* published in 1933 and 1939, respectively.[5]

According to Fisher's classification method, primary production includes agriculture, forestry, fishery and hunting; secondary production includes mining, manufacturing, construction, transportation and communication, and public utilities (e.g., electricity and gas); and tertiary production covers public services such as commerce, finance, catering, and public administrative affairs such as science, education, culture, health, and government. Production is classified by consumption demand. Assuming that maximum consumer demand is 1, then production with consumer demand < 0.5 is classified to be primary, consumer demand between 0.5 and 1 to be secondary, and equal to 1 to be tertiary.

The greatest contribution from Fisher's theory was the introduction of the three-sector model, from which industrial structure theories began to take shape.

IV. *Florence's Theory of Industrial Development*

Almost at the same time as Fisher, P. S. Florence examined industrial development from the perspective of economic structure.[6] He believed that economic (industrial) development has the following five characteristics: i) The labor force shift from agriculture to manufacturing and services; ii) Increase in the quantity as well as the integration of capital; iii) Increase of professionals in various industrial sectors; iv) Expansion of market and supply resources; and v) Diversification of manufacturing.

This process sees the advancement of industrial structure and the expansion and concentration of industrial organizations, mainly manifested in i) Larger plant size; ii) More horse power per worker; and iii) Higher degree of localization. Along with economic development, the characteristics of industrial mechanization, transportation mechanization, and high-speed information transmission become increasingly prominent. This tendency is, in many industries, accompanied by the expansion of enterprise size, growth in industrial integration, and concentration of industrial location and urbanization.

It is obvious that Florence already discovered and partly summarized the transfer of labor force between sectors as proposed by Colin Clark, however his research did not receive enough attention from academia.

Section 2   Initial Formation

The theoretical paradigm of industrial structure was formed in the 1940s, but it did not become applicable worldwide until the 1960s. After being empirically proved by Simon Kuznets and H. B. Chenery, Clark's Law was deemed almost infallible.

I.   Clark's Law

Colin Clark carried on Petty and Fisher's views, and through systematic organization, set up a complete, systematic theoretical framework of industrial structure – Clark's Law. In the 9th chapter – "Distribution of Labor Force Among Sectors" – of his book *The Conditions of Economic Progress* published in 1940, Clark discussed the most important symbiotic phenomenon of economic development: the transfer of the labor force from the agricultural sector to the manufacturing sector, and afterwards to the commercial and service sectors.[7]

Clark's theory has three premises: i) It is based on the changes in individual economies over a time series. The time series represents economic development, which therein represents the increase of national income; ii) Labor force is used for the first time as an indicator to examine its changes in distribution among various sectors in the process of economic development; and iii) The economy is divided by Fisher's three-sector classification method. To be more specific, the primary sector encompasses agriculture, animal husbandry, fishery, forestry, and hunting. The secondary sector includes mining, manufacturing, construction, and public utilities (e.g., electricity). The tertiary sector covers commerce, transportation, administration, household services and other non-material production. As such, Clark ascertained that a law, with respect to the relationship between economic development and industrial structure evolution, exists.

Firstly, international comparisons show that, (although there are exceptions) countries with a higher per capita national income generally have a lower employment-to-population ratio (EPR) in the primary sector; whereas in countries with a lower per capita national income, this ratio is higher. The higher the national income, the larger EPR in services, and vice versa. Secondly, almost without exception, EPR tends to decrease in the primary sector and to increase in the service sector, and remains unchanged or grows slightly in the secondary sector, as indicated by the historical trajectories of economic development.

Similarly, if the proportion of income is used to examine industrial structure, the same conclusions can be drawn. On an international scale, in countries with a higher per capita national income, the primary sector accounts for a smaller proportion of income compared to the secondary and tertiary sectors. Conclusions are almost identical if examined in chronological order. But the EPR growth rate of the secondary sector is limited, while the proportion of income tends to climb obviously for the secondary sector and slightly for the tertiary sector. This is because labor productivity increases significantly in secondary industries, i.e., manufacturing, where labor is not too intensive. In other words, improving labor productivity through machinery is more prominent in the secondary industry. Therefore, it is more appropriate to examine this sector by income and the tertiary sector by employment.

In the 4th chapter – "Distribution of Labor Force Among Sectors" – Clark tracked the economic growth of multiple countries based on long-term data. Among them, quite long data segments were used for the United States (1820–1950), Australia (1871–1947), Denmark (1834–1952), France (1827–1951), Germany (1882–1950), Great Britain (1841–1951), India (1881–1951), Ireland (1841–1946), Italy (1871–1951), Japan (1872–1950), New Zealand (1861–1945), Norway (1875–1950), Sweden (1840–1950), and Switzerland (1880–1941).

Throughout this investigation, Clark proposed his famous theory of industrial structure: under normal circumstances, the ratio of both employment and income transfers from the primary to the secondary sector, and afterwards to the tertiary sector when national income is further increased. Clark believed his research findings only proved Petty's thesis, thus, Clark's Law is also called Petty-Clark's Law.

II. Theoretical Confirmation by Kuznets

Simon Kuznets carried on and further refined Clark's study. He analyzed trends in the distribution of national income among the three sectors, and discussed the causes of industrial structure evolution. His main research findings are described in *Modern Economic Growth: Rate, Structure and Spread*.[8]

First, on the theoretical premise, Kuznets changed Clark's "time series" into "economic growth" as an explicit concept, that is, there will be continuous population increase on the condition that per capita product does not decrease obviously. Simultaneously, the increase of population and per capita product are indispensable. Here, "continuous increase" refers to a substantial increase that will not disappear because of short-term changes.

Second, on industrial classification, Kuznets referred to the primary, secondary, and tertiary sectors as the agricultural, industrial, and service sectors, respectively (also adopted in this study). Specifically, A (agricultural) sector includes agriculture, forestry, and fishery; I (industrial) sector includes mining, manufacturing, construction, electricity, transportation and communications, etc.; S (service) sector includes commerce, finance, real estate, personal, corporate, and household experts, and government services. From the perspective of time series (the long-run), the following conclusions can be drawn:

1. The national income realized by agriculture declines contin-uously as a proportion of the gross national income (relative share of national income) over time, in the same manner as the proportion of agricultural labor decreases in the gross labor force (relative share of labor force).

2. The relative share of national income of the industrial sector generally rises, whereas the relative share of the labor force remains largely unchanged or increases in various countries.

3. The relative share of the labor force of services increases in almost all countries, while the relative share of national income may not necessarily be synchronized, but generally is roughly unchanged or slightly increased.

There is a slight difference between cross-sectional analysis and time series analysis. For example, the relative share of labor of industry is roughly unchanged in the time series analysis, while it increases in the cross-sectional analysis.

Third, Kuznets used the concept of relative national income to further examine industrial structure. This refers to a sector's relative share of national income compared to its relative share of labor force – comparative labor productivity. Therefore, the following conclusions can be drawn:

1. The relative national income of the agricultural sector is less than 1 in most countries, which is contrary to the results in industry and services. In view of this, a decreasing agricultural labor force in most countries has become the norm.
2. The relative share of the industrial labor force varies among countries due to differences in industrialization level. In short, it is slightly increased or unchanged. However, the relative share of national income generally rises in the industrial sector alone.
3. The relative national income of the service sector usually decreases, but the relative share of the labor force is rising. In general, the relative share is more than 50% in terms of both labor and national income.

Unlike Clark, Kuznets adopted a different time series for data analysis by comparing the early and late periods of segmented data of major countries. Specifically, the main data series covers the periods as follows:

- United Kingdom: 1) England and Wales, national income (NI), 1688–1770; 2) Great Britain, NI, 1801–1841; 3) Great Britain, NI, 1841–1901; 4) Great Britain, NI, 1907–1924; 5) United Kingdom, gross national product (GNP), 1924–1955.
- France: 6) NI, 1789/1815–1825/1835; 7) NI, 1825/1835–1872/1882; 8) NI, 1872/1882–1908/1910; 9) gross domestic product (GNP), 1954–1962.
- Germany: 10) 1913 German Empire, NI, 1860/1869–1905/1914; 11) the Federal Republic, GDP, 1936–1959.
- Holland: 12) NI, 1913–1938; 13) GDP, 1950–1962.
- Denmark: Net domestic product (NDP), 14) at current prices, 1870/1874–1905/1909; 15) at current prices, 1905/1909–1948/1952; 16) at 1929 prices, 1870/1874–1905/1909; 17) at 1929 prices, 1905/1909–1948/1952.
- Norway: 18) GDP, 1865–1910; 19) GDP, 1910–1956.
- Sweden: 20) GDP, 1861/1865–1901/1905; 21) GDP, 1901/1905–1949/1953.
- Italy: 22) NI, 1861/1865–1896/1900; 23) NI, 1896/1900–1951/1955.
- United States: Commodity production, 1839–1879, 24) at current price; 25) at 1879 prices. NI and trading volume, 26) at current prices, 1869/1879–1919/1928; 27) at current prices, 1919/1928–1939/1948; 28) at 1929 prices, 1869/1878–1939/1948; 29) at current prices, 1929–1961/1963.
- Canada: 30) GNP, 1870–1920; 31) GDP, 1926/1928–

1961/1963; 32) GDP, at 1949 prices, 1926/1928–1953/1955.

- Australia: GDP, 1861/1865–1934/1935–1938/1939, 33) at current prices; 34) at 1910/1911 prices.
- Japan: 35) NDP, 1878/1882–1923/1927; 36) NDP, 1950–1962.
- Soviet Union: 37) NDP, at factor prices in 1937, 1928–1958.[9]

To sum up, Kuznets rearranged the basic framework of theories on industrial structure to make it more sophisticated. His theory enriched research methods and made theories on industrial structure more robust and accurate.

III. Theoretical Confirmation by Chenery

Chenery (1986) proved that the level of economic development is intrinsically linked to the share of tertiary industry in the industrial structure.[10] His theoretical contributions with respect to the law on industrial evolution are mainly as follows:

Firstly, on the research framework for industrial structure, Chenery further enriched existing theories by replacing the concept of "industrial structure" with "economic structure." "The structure of an economy can be defined by its production factors – labor, capital, and natural resources – and their employment in different uses or sectors. The term structural transformation encompasses "the changes in economic structure that led to, and are caused by, a rise in the national product, together with the proximate causes of these changes."[11]

Secondly, on the basic measure of economic structure, Chenery shifted from Clark's labor force to "the share of gross net product originating in each sector of the economy."[12]

Thirdly, on basic conclusions of economic structure, Chenery noticed that industry grew quickly in sample countries from the 1950–70s after WWII. He stressed that, confirming Clark and Kuznets' studies, "The most notable feature of structural transformation is the rise in the share of manufacturing in gross national product and the corresponding decline in the share of agriculture." "The rise of employment in industry is much smaller than the decline in agriculture, and consequently most of the shift takes place from agriculture to services,"[13] which carried forward Clark's basic view.

Fourthly, on specific sector classification, Chenery divided the economy into four sectors. Among them, primary products and manufacturing (subdivided into light industry and heavy industry) are tradable sectors; and social overhead and services are non-tradable sectors. If primary products correspond to the primary sector and manufacturing to the secondary sector, the rest falls into the tertiary sector. This method is roughly equivalent to sector classification based on the narrower definition of industrial sector.[14]

Fifth, in terms of data collection, Chenery adopted the methodology of multi-country comparative analysis (which is also the purpose and feature of the book). He used the data series of the following nine economies to examine changes in related indicators in the early and late periods. The specific countries and periods covered by the study are as follows:

15

Colombia, 1953–1970; Mexico, 1950–1975; Turkey, 1953–1973; Yugoslavia, 1962–1972; Japan, 1955–1970; Korea, 1955–1973; China Taiwan, 1956–1971; Israel, 1958–1972; Norway, 1953–1969.[15]

In summary, Chenery's study on industrial structure went a step further, but still failed to escape the pitfall of Clark's Law. He inherited the mantle of Clark's Law while shifting the perspective to the share of gross net product. Chenery found that there was an obvious increase in gross domestic product share of the industrial sector during the study period. Nevertheless, misled by the phenomenon that the service sector basically dominates developed economies, Chenery effectively became an interpreter of Clark's Law.

Section 3   Extension of Clark's Law

In the aftermath of the stagflation crisis in the 1970s, new changes seemed to provide real evidence for Clark and Kuznets' thesis on industrial structure. In this regard, Western economists extended Clark's Law beyond the 70s and proposed the theory of post-industrial society. Here, "post-industrial society" refers to an economy in which the industrial share keeps declining while that of the service sector keeps rising. It denotes that economic society has passed the industrial stage, and thus industrial society has come to an end.

I. Machlup's Theory of Knowledge Industry

Ever since the 1960s, the share of the industrial sector has declined in developed capitalist countries such as the United States. Fritz Machlup was the earliest to realize or conclude this shift from the industrial age to the next exists. In 1962, he conducted a special study on the production and distribution of "knowledge."[16]

Machlup proposed an economic analysis of the production of knowledge for the following reasons: i) Increasing shares of the nation's budget have been allocated to production of knowledge; ii) A large portion of the nation's expenditure on knowledge has been financed by the government; iii) The production of knowledge yields social benefits in excess of private benefits accruing to the recipients of knowledge; iv) The production of certain kinds of knowledge is limited by inelasticities in the supply of qualified labor; v) The fact that production of knowledge of several types is paid for by others rather than users of the knowledge and that these types of knowledge have market prices, raises questions of valuation for national-income accounting as well as for welfare-economic considerations; vi) The production of one type of knowledge, namely technology, results in continuing changes in the conditions of production of many goods and services; vii) New technical knowledge tends to result in shifts of demand from physical labor to brain workers; viii) There is an increase in the share of knowledge-producing labor in total employment in the United States; ix) There is ground for suspicion that some branches of the production of knowledge are quite inefficient; x) Some of the growth in the production of knowledge may be an instance of Parkinson's Law; and xi) The increase in the ratio of knowledge-producing labor to physical labor is strongly associated with the increase in productivity and thus with the rate of economic growth.

Machlup distinguished five types of knowledge: i) Practical knowledge (professional, business, workman's, political, household, and other practical knowledge.); ii) Intellectual knowledge: iii) Small-talk and pastime knowledge; iv) Spiritual knowledge; and v) Unwanted knowledge. The knowledge industry can also be classified into five categories: i) Education; ii) Research & development; iii) Media and communication; iv) information machines; and v) Information services. Furthermore, knowledge is divided by use into intermediate products and final outputs. The former is measured by the cost of production, and the latter is subdivided into investment and consumption. Machlup analyzed the knowledge industry from an economic perspective. His study had a relatively far-reaching impact, although the definitions and statistical methods he used are debatable.

II. *Bell's Theory of Post-industrial Society*

Sociologist Daniel Bell said in his work *The Coming of Post-Industrial Society* that economic society is entering a new era – post-industrial society.[17] He examined social development at two levels: ownership and technology. Along the trajectory of ownership, there are traditional development models: feudalist, capitalist, and socialist society; and along the trajectory of technology or knowledge, there are pre-industrial, industrial, and post-industrial society.

Bell summed up the five dimensions of post-industrial society: i) Economic sector: the transition from a manufacturing to a service economy; ii) Occupational change: the rise of professional and technical classes; iii) Axial principle: the centrality of theoretical knowledge, owning to technological innovation and policy decision-making; vi) Future direction: technology management and technology valuation; and v) Decision making: the creation of new "intellectual technology." Bell emphasized the primacy of technical knowledge, around which new technology, economic prosperity, and social organization can be formed. The axial principle proposes that advanced industrial society shows an increased tendency to become dominant.

Bell said the earliest and simplest feature of post-industrial society is that most labor is not engaged in agriculture or manufacturing, but in services. He divided services into four categories: i) Personal services (retail stores, laundries, car repair, beauty salons, etc.); ii) Practical services (banks and credit unions, real estate, insurance); iii) Transportation, communication, and public utilities; and iv) Health, education, research, and governance. Among them, the quaternary sector has played a decisive role in the arrival of post-industrial society, which is manifested in the rise of universities, research institutions, professional classes, and government departments. From the perspective of occupational structure, in 1956, white-collar workers outnumbered blue-collar workers in the United States – the first time ever in the history of industrial civilization. Professional and technical classes required by university education expanded at a rate more than twice the average, of which scientists and technicians grew at a rate of three times the average.

There are considerable differences among pre-industrial, industrial, and post-industrial societies defined by Bell, as shown in Table 1.1. The social composition, economic, and occupational structures vary widely, depending on the basis of each society. For example, the core issue of industrial society lies in capital, that is, how to institutionalize the process of creating sufficient savings and how to channel these funds to investment fields. Social relations lie within enterprises, and social issues are mainly labor disputes. But when the investment process is stabilized, class struggle will be suppressed to a certain extent, thus class conflict will not divide society.

Correspondingly, the primary problem of post-industrial society is the organization of science – research is mainly conducted by universities and research institutions. In the 19th and early 20th centuries, so-called national power was industrial capacity, measured mainly by steel production. After WWII, technological capacity became the decisive factor of potential and actual national strength; research & development has replaced steel yields as a measure of national strength. Therefore, the nature and type of state support for science, the politicization of science, the organization of scientific group research, and social factors are all major policy issues in post-industrial society.

Politically speaking, the problem of post-industrial society is the inadequate development of a non-market welfare economy and the lack of an appropriate mechanism to determine the distribution of public goods. From a technical or conceptual

Table 1.1 Bell's Pattern of Social Development

Classification	Pre-industrial society	Industrial society	Post-industrial society
Region	Asia, Africa, Latin America	Western Europe, Soviet Union, Japan	United States
Economic sector	Primary sector: agriculture, mining, fishery, forestry	Secondary sector material production: manufacturing, processing	Tertiary sector: transportation, public welfare Quaternary sector: trade, finance, insurance, real estate Quinary sector: health, education, research, government, entertainment
Professional orientation	Farmers, miners, fishermen, unskilled workers	Semi-skilled workers, technicians	Professional technicians, scientists
Technology	Raw materials	Energy	Information
Composition principle	Management of nature	Management of man-made nature	Interpersonal management
Methods	Common sense, experience	Empiricism, experimentation	Abstract theories: model, simulation, experiment, decision theory, system analysis
Outlook	Past ambitions, specific countermeasures	Specific adaptation, planning	Future ambitions and predictions
Basic principle	Traditionalism: scarcity of land and resources	Economic growth: state or individual management of investment	The primacy of theoretical knowledge and the formation of knowledge culture

Source: Ruyu Zhao, *Post-industrial Society Parallelism Changchun* (Jilin People's Publishing House, 1999), 14.

point of view, the value of such goods cannot be measured by the market. Moreover, since public goods are distributed to all citizens, this kind of expenditure fails to obtain strong support from citizens. Most importantly, the non-market nature of such goods, that rely on political decision-making, becomes a typical source of disputes. The rise in political awareness intensifies people's requirements for equality and engagement, whereas the demand for specialists proficient in modern knowledge is also increasing. As long as intellectual technology-based decision-making is carried out, stronger planning and order than ever before will be required. In this way, there is bound to be a fierce conflict between the fundamental and indispensable morality that supports the post-industrial society, and the various desires for self-realization in this new society. Cultural contradictions constitute the most profound issue that determines survival of this new society.

Section 4   Offshoots of Industrial Structure Theories

Apart from the aforementioned theories of Western economists on industrial structure, the theoretical views of two economists, as an offshoot of these, also deserve a mention.

I.   *Schumpeter's Theory of Innovation*

J. A. Schumpeter said in his book *Theory of Economic Development* published in 1912 that the capitalist process is the combined result of cyclical passive adaptation and active innovation with which industrial structure, capital structure and trade structure all have a certain corresponding relationship. The transformative force in the cycle of passive adaptation that changes the economy inside is innovation.[18]

Specifically, innovation covers the following five aspects: i) Production of new products unknown to consumers; ii) Introduction of new technologies to existing products; iii) Expansion of new markets; iv) Development of new materials and new resources; and v) Establishment of new organizations. Among them, i), ii) and iii) are important factors that determine industrial structure; ii) and v) are essential factors that change the capital structure of industries; iii) and iv) are decisive factors that determine trade structure. Entrepreneurs seek increased profits by combining these factors; then they can expand credit from financial institutions through technological innovations, while financial institutions provide entrepreneurs with a large amount of funds that exceed savings. In this way, close links will be forged between entrepreneurs and banks, in which technological innovation serves as a medium to drive the development of industrial society. This process is defined as "creative destruction." Here, as the executor of technological innovation, entrepreneurs introduce new ideas into the material production process and put them into practice, that is, entrepreneurship.

On the whole, the theory of innovation has a very close relationship with industrial development and long-term fluctuations of industrial structure, which can explain the evolution mechanism of industrial structure in a more far-reaching sense.

II. Kondratieff's Theory of Long Waves

N. D. Kondratieff said in a 1925 paper that price changes in an irregular sinusoidal form while output changes only in growth rate. As output changes, price shows the characteristic of pro-cyclical changes: Rapid economic growth accompanies inflation and slow economic growth accompanies deflation.[19]

Kondratieff thus emphasized the long cycles of economic activities, and tried to use this theory to explain the long waves of price and output. The long cycles are as specified in Table 1.2.

Kondratieff further described long wave characteristics by pointing out five salient features worthy of attention: i) Boom years represent most of the long-term upswing phase, and depression years represent most of the long-term downswing phase; ii) Agricultural problems are particularly significant in the downswing phase of long waves; iii) In the downswing phase, inventions emerge endlessly and will be applied on a large scale in

Table 1.2   Kondratieff's Long Cycles

Long wave	Feature	Start time	End time
First long wave	Rise	The 1780s	1810–1817
	Decline	1810–1817	1844–1851
Second long wave	Rise	1844–1851	1870–1875
	Decline	1870–1875	1890–1896
Third long wave	Rise	1890–1896	1914–1920
	Decline	1914–1920	–

Source: John Eatwell et al., *The New Palgrave Dictionary of Economics* (Beijing: Economic Science Press, 1996), 61–62.

the upswing phase of the next long wave; iv) In the early upswing phase, gold production will increase, and the world commodity market will expand with the addition of new countries, especially colonial countries; and v) Wars and revolutions often take place in the upswing phase.

Kondratieff's theory of long waves is an exploratory summary of long economic development cycles. It has a certain significance with respect to the endogenous cycles of economic activities, especially the long cycles of industrial revolution. However, constrained by price fluctuations, this theory is questioned because it fails to examine the long cycles of industrial revolution beyond the general cycles of industrial production. Of course, this is also related with historical limitations. Kondratieff investigated economic activities that happened to be at a low point of the long-term economic cycle under the impact of the Second Industrial Revolution only. Thus, his conclusions are drawn from limited observations.

Notes

1. William Petty, *Political Arithmetick*, trans. CHEN Dongye (Beijing: The Commercial Press, 1978), 19–20.

2. Karl Marx, *A Contribution to the Critique of Political Economy*, vol. 18, *Karl Marx Frederick Engels Collected Works* (Beijing: People's Publishing House, 1976), 43.

3. Karl Marx, and Frederick Engels, vol. 20, *Karl Marx Frederick Engels Collected Works* (Beijing: People's Publishing House, 1976), 255.

4. Adam Smith, *An Inquiry into the Nature and Causes of the Wealth of Nation* (Oxford: Clarendon Press, 1976).

5. A. G. Fisher, "Capital and the Growth of Knowledge," *Economic Journal* no. 9 (1933); A. G. Fisher, "Production, Primary, Secondary, and Tertiary," *Economic Record,* no. 6 (1939).

6. P. S. Florence, *The Logic of British and American Industry: A Realistic Analysis of Economic Structure and Government* (London: Routedge & Keganpaul Ltd, 1935).

7. C. Clark, *The Conditions of Economic Progress (3rd Edition)* (London: Macmillan; New York: St. Martin's Press, 1957).

8. Simon Kuznets, *Modem Economic Growth: Rate, Structure and Spread* (Yale University Press, 1966).

9. Ibid., 88–94.

10. Hollis B. Chenery, Sherman Robinson, and Moshe Syrquin, *Industrialization and Growth: A Comparative Study* (Oxford University Press, 1986), 84–118.

11. Hollis B. Chenery, Sherman Robinson, and Moshe Syrquin, *Industrialization and Growth: A Comparative Study*, tans. WU Qi et al. (Shanghai: Shanghai Joint Publishing Press, 1995), 57.

12. Ibid., 58.

13. Ibid., 59, 90.

14. Ibid., 59, 64.

15. Ibid., 59, 80–120.

16. F. Machlup, *The Production and Distribution of Knowledge in the United States* (Princeton: N. Y. Princeton University Press, 1962).

17. D. Bell, *The Coming of Post-Industrial Society* (New York: Basic Books, 1973).

18. J. A. Schumpeter, *Theorie der Wirschaftlichen Entwicklung* (Leipzig, Grermany: Dunker & Humblot, 1912).

19. N. D. Kondratieff, "The Major Economic Cycles," *Vorosy, Kon' iunknry* no. 1, (1925): 28–79.

CHAPTER 2

Defects of Clark's Theoretical Paradigm

A theoretical paradigm mainly consists of three parts: the premise, deductive logic based on premise, and conclusions. Generally, we identify the defects of a theoretical paradigm by first noticing a deviation of its conclusions from reality, and then reflecting on its premises and logic. However, Clark's Law is fundamentally wrong in these critical areas, which leads to erroneous conclusions.

Section 1   Realistic Glory and Rejection

Clark's Law has been empirically proven by many Nobel Prize-winning theorists, giving it the aura of an "iron law." On the one hand, from its emergence to the exposure of its theoretical flaws, this theory was rooted in the long-cycle of the Third Industrial Revolution. In this cycle, most developed economies saw an increase in the share of services. On the other hand, in a globally integrated industrial system, the service sector of developed countries greatly benefited from the industrial contributions of newly industrialized countries, creating the illusion of prosperity. Consequently, the virtual economy over expanded in developed nations, occupying an unusually high proportion of the total economy. Global advancement of industrial technology was too slow to support this huge service sector. It was not until this historical departure from reality was exposed in the form of the Japanese economic crisis – beginning in the 1980s, then the Asian financial crisis, and the US subprime mortgage crisis that the flaws in Clark's Law have become clearer.

I. *Theoretical Glory*

Theories on industrial structure have been around more than 300 years now. In this process – which is nearly 100 years longer than the history of industrial society – these theories have deepened our understanding of the objective world, though they are mostly author descriptions or empirical analysis of the objective reality in their era. Many viewpoints are of practical significance and value, in addition to academic value, and have played a positive role in the development of modern industrial society. In this regard, they must be evaluated from the perspective of historical materialism.

In terms of academia, the introduction and development of hypotheses in industrial structure has expanded economic theory through more rigorous methods, more accurate conclusions, and gradually deepened analysis, providing a theoretical basis for actual industrial structure.

Firstly, these theories have enriched theoretical economic systems. The economy of a country, in essence, is generally composed of the national economy, the industrial economy and the corporate economy – in other words, the macro-, meso-, and micro-economies. Economics, which reflects the theoretical form of economy, should also comprise these three parts.

Secondly, these theories have supplemented economic development theory: evolution of industrial structure is one of the most important features manifested in the process of economic development. Therefore, theories on industrial structure, which were pioneered by Clark, are also important. Carrying forward his thoughts, Kuznets and Shinohara adapted these theories to be more sophisticated and practical. After the 1970s, Machlup, Bell, Toffler, and others expanded the connotation of productivity and further emphasized the importance of technology (knowledge) and technological revolution in economic development.

Thirdly, theories on industrial structure have explored new research methods. In early and even current economic studies, there are many theories far detached from reality. Even worse, some theories fabricate examples completely out of thin air; a typical case is Ricardo's theory. Ricardian economics made predictions on the increasing costs of growing grain, mounting population pressures on food supply, rising share of landlords' income, and gradual disappearance of investment opportunities. These predictions narrow the differences between abstract conclusions and specific applications, so it is difficult to determine whether they are an unconditional historical forecast or a conditional trend statement. Ricardo told the British Parliament that some economic conclusions are as irrefutable as the law of gravity. At the same time, he told Malthus that he fabricated some powerful examples to explain principles and illustrate their effects. This kind of theory, of course, cannot guide reality.

Since their formation, these theories on industrial structure have employed economic statistics as an evidence, which is a feature of their research methodology. Petty (1676) is considered the forefather of econometrics because of his work *Political Arithmetic*. With the establishment of the three-sector classification method, economic statistics has become more sophisticated and detailed.

Kuznets (1966) made a statistical regression analysis of the panel data and long-term historical data of more than 50 countries, examining the transformation in industrial structure on different periods of aggregate growth. Chenery (1986) used the input-output model, general equilibrium analysis, and econometric models to further analyze the relationship between per capita income and industrial structure of low-income countries, the effect of domestic demand, foreign trade, and production technology on structural changes, and the influence of each sector and factor on economic growth at different stages. The author, Ruyu Zhao (1999, 2013), focused on the relationship between the economic growth rate and industrial structure. These methods and advances paved a path for in-depth research in related fields. In terms of practical guidance, theories on industrial structure offer a methodical way of thinking about economic development. Especially in the post-war era after 1945, structural thinking has inspired new ideas on industrial choice and crisis management.

Firstly, these theories are academically based on economic reality and directly serve economic reality. They offer new insights and a richer theoretical basis for formulating economic policies. In the aftermath of WWII, the application of industrial structure theories has become more common, for example in Japan, which realized post-war high-speed growth.

Secondly, they provide a theoretical basis for economic development breakthroughs. In 1957, Miyohei Shinohara published a paper entitled "Industrial Structure and Investment Allocation" in the Hitotsubashi University journal *Economic Research*. This famous Japanese industrial economist set the benchmarks in the planning of Japan's industrial structure – known as Shinohara Benchmarks, which includes benchmarks for income elasticity and productivity improvement. His theory summarized the law of industrial structure development at a time when heavy chemical industries occupied a dominant share. This played a direct guiding role in the formulation of industrial policies and the choice of leading industries in Japan.

In addition, Miyazawa Kenichi (1963, 1966) applied the theory of industrial linkage to structural analysis and causal analysis, which supplied a theoretical basis for the formulation of economic plans and industrial policies. Sanuki Toshio (1981), Umaba Masao (1974), and Komiya Ryutaro (1964, 1975, 1984) also conducted comprehensive analyses of industrial structure concentration and industrial organization. Guided by these, the Japanese government began to formulate and adjust industrial policies in the 1950s to foster leading industry and exports, thereby creating an economic growth miracle.

Thirdly, theories on industrial structure propose legitimate ways to improve the quality and efficiency of national economy. Arguments on upgrading industrial structure and the role of technological revolution imply a transition from labor-intensive to capital-intensive industries, putting knowledge-intensive industries at the forefront of the nation's economy. Therefore, the practical significance of theories on industrial structure cannot be denied.

II. *Historical Limitations*

Economics realizes theoretical sublimation by summarizing the course of economic development. Hence, every explorer of economic theories can only conduct work in their own historical context on the basis of existing research. This leads to historical and cognitive limitations of all explorers of economic theories. The theories of industrial structure have played an important role in academia and practice so far, however they are inevitably defective. For example, Fisher, Clark, Kuznets, and Chenery employed different methods for industrial classification and analyzed issues from different perspectives due to their temporal and spatial differences. Japan has its own classification standards:

specifically, the tertiary industry includes transportation and communication, electricity, gas, water, service, and public affairs. However, these would normally be considered to be part of the secondary sector. Such differences and ambiguity indicates the theoretical framework is still imperfect. More importantly, these theories are being fundamentally challenged with societal progress.

The challenge arises from the historical limitations of those who proposed and followed Clark's Law. This is reflected in two aspects: i) They cannot rid the influence of their historical period on their ways of thinking. They ignored the periodicity of economic activities themselves and failed to notice the significance of long cycles of industrial revolutions; and ii) The research methodology and theoretical logic went against basic economic principles. These researchers used labor force share to signal gross domestic product (GDP) trends, built false premises on absolute economic growth – on this basis, they created the absolute truth known as the "time function." These fallacies have become accepted as standards, and the objectives of economics – the realization of optimal allocation, as well as human nature – forgotten in the pursuit of economic growth. To artificially prove the existence of a certain law, they abandon their initiative and take a laissez-faire attitude to economic recession to satisfy this hypothesis.

Section 2   The Absurdity of Petty's Law

Behind traditional theories on industrial structure lies theoretical dogma as Western economists have been influenced by historical limits, as well as limits in their way of thinking. However, such conclusions have been become ultimate truths – called the Law.

I.   *Limitations of Research Horizons*

Petty's preliminary conclusion is deduced, solely, from prosperous early maritime trade brought about by the Age of Discovery; it has little to do with the evolution of industrial society. In the early days of the British Industrial Revolution, industry was still underdeveloped and agriculture was not strong enough to support it, which is where Smith drew his conclusions. Clark adopted a wider perspective by using data from the start of industrialization to the late 1930s and even 1940s. Nonetheless, this period still only covered the Second Industrial Revolution. Not unexpectedly, the results affect overarching theories on industrial structure, and by extension the entire economic growth process.

Kuznets drew on data up to the 1960s, when the Third Industrial Revolution had not been fully realized, thus, there is no evident difference in the research periods between Kuznets and Clark. Meanwhile, Chenery essentially failed to deviate from Kuznets' method: his study recognized traditional theories as central tenets, though extended research to the 1970s. Later, theories on post-industrial society focused on the crisis of Western economies and the tendency of service sector domination after the 1970s; this is biased to a certain extent. Such limitations directly lead to one-sided conclusions. If including the First Industrial Revolution in research, it is not difficult to find that fluctuations in the share of secondary and tertiary industries are not continuous but cyclical.

II. Fallacy of Theoretical Premises

As mentioned above, historical limitations are partly to blame for the flawed conclusion drawn – that dominance of the tertiary industry is an inevitable trend of economic and social development. In fact, the defects of the theoretical premise also make the conclusions unscientific.

The core premise of traditional theories on industrial structure is the precondition of economic development. In Clark's view, economic development equals the time series. This is based on the changes of individual economies over time; time represents economic development. Therein, economic development represents the continuous increase of national income. This view of economic development makes Clark's Law an absolute truth that coexists with time.

In this regard, Kuznets sensed the time limitations of Clark's study and used economic growth instead, that is, the continuous increase of population under the condition that per capita product does not decrease obviously – in other words, it increases or does not change. Simultaneously, population increase and per capita product increase are indispensable. Here, "continuous increase" refers to the obvious improvement that will not disappear due to short-term change. Although it is logical, this definition assumes absolute truth, which is not applicable in reality. According to the United Nations, in the last 200 years – of which we have statistical data – almost every country has realized population growth with per capita product increasing or staying the same in a relatively long historical period.[1] That is to say, in reality, the term "economic growth" used by Kuznets still equals time. Naturally, the law of evolution of industrial structure, further proved by Kuznets, also has the aura of absolute truth.

As we know, since the world is unlimited and human cognition is limited, there is no absolute truth. Moreover, traditional theories that take the time series as a presupposition ignore the fluctuations of economic growth in the short and even long term. Simply based on the transformation of industrial structure in certain historical periods, they reach incomplete conclusions on economic and social trends with regards to the tertiary sector.

III. *Absurdity of Theoretical Logic*

The failure of traditional industrial structure theories represented by Clark's Law is largely reflected in three aspects: classification standards for industries; indicators of industrial structure, and poor data usage. Among them, the use of national income to examine economic growth is a major error.

Firstly, industrial classification standards was first raised by Fisher. He used the elasticity of consumption demand specific to industry as the criterion for industrial stricture. On this basis, Clark and Kuznets[2] both set up classification standards. These classifications are more or less the same – their difference lies in whether some public utilities, such as transportation and

Table 2.1   Comparison of traditional classifications of
industrial structure

Division mode	Fischer	Clark	Kuznets
Primary industry	Agriculture, forestry, fishery and hunting	Agriculture, animal husbandry, fishery, forestry and hunting	Agricultural and aquatic products
Secondary industry	Mining, manufacturing, construction, power and gas and other public utilities	Mining, manufacturing, construction, public utilities and power	Mining, manufacturing, construction, power, transportation, post and telecommunications, communication and others
Tertiary industry	Public services such as commerce, finance, catering and public administrative services such as science, education, culture, health and government	Commerce, transportation, administration, family services and other industries of immaterial production	Commerce, finance, real estate, individuals, enterprises, family services, professional services and government services

Source: Compiled by the author based on relevant studies.

communication, and water and gas, fall in the secondary or tertiary sector. Such inconsistency in classification has made the basis of industrial structure ambiguous; these specific classifications are shown in Table 2.1.

Secondly, Clark's Law used labor force as the indicator when examining changes in the distribution of labor during economic development. This is contradictory to using national income to indicate economic development: i) The dominant indicator of economic growth is GDP or national income, while the distribution of labor force among industries does not have an intrinsic link to GDP or national income. Per capita national income is not equal to per capita income of labor. It is obvious that the price of labor varies across different industries. ii) According to the labor theory of value, as labor creates value, working hours can be taken as an indicator to measure product value or product price. However, even though working hours in different industries were the same, the employment level of a certain industry could not be the measurement of the value created by it; employment scale cannot completely represent labor value. Land of the primary industry, machines of the secondary industry, and equipment of the tertiary industry are all materialized forms of laboring. Their value cannot be embodied in the amount of employment; iii) Even though employment in different industries was the same, effective division of the labor force could promote productivity, which leads to differences in value created in different industries; such differences cannot be calculated by the amount of employment.

Thirdly, data analysis by Clark, Kuznets, and Chenery is limited to the simple examination of change in time segments. As noted earlier, Clark tracked the economic growth of multiple countries and regions in his chapter "Distribution of Labor Force Among Industries." However, emphasis was put on data change between early and later periods, such as analysis on the United States (1820–1950), Australia (1971–1947), Denmark (1834–1952), France (1827–1951), Germany (1882–1950), and Great Britain (1841–1951).

Kuznets used a different time series from Clark. He examined economic growth change between early and later periods over a longer time series, however this is a refined version of Clark's approach, with no essential progress in methodology.

Chenery also adopted a similar method to examine data segments of nine economies, but his approach was a step backwards compared to Kuznets: i) Only periods from the 1950s to 1970s were examined; and ii) The economies covered were not representative industrialized countries, but emerging industrialized countries or regions, such as Colombia, Mexico, Turkey, and Yugoslavia.

IV. Neglect of the Open Economy

Traditional scholars conducted research on a country basis because of data restrictions. Yet, this reflects a lack of understanding of change in industrial structure brought about by international economic cooperation.

It is undeniable that, with the considerable advancement of open economy after WWII, transformation in industrial structure of a country no longer has an independent, closed, and causal relationship with economic growth. In an open economy, the industrial structure of a country or region is inseparable from the international economic cycle. The industrial structures of various countries will form a large supranational community-style industrial structure that depends on the material production sector (secondary industry in the industrial society) as a whole to drive forward economic development. As the industries in any one country only form part of the world economy, the industrial structure of some countries may be dominated by a particular sector.

In the United States, for example, the tertiary industry has represented a higher share than both the primary and secondary industries since industrialization – it is dominated by the tertiary sector. However, as the US is deeply connected to the global economy and international division of labor, it is not appropriate to simply conclude that it has reached post-industrial society just because of the high share of tertiary industry. Similarly, it is inappropriate to deduce that American economic growth is driven by the tertiary industry. In fact, through empirical research in the following chapters, we will show that the secondary industry still plays a key role in long-term economic growth. The United States is not only influenced by the growth of the secondary industry of other countries, but also directly affected by the fluctuations of its domestic secondary industry. As the US has led the world economy since WWII, the prosperity and decline of its secondary industry will affect other closely related economies, thereby exerting a far-reaching impact on the global economy.

To sum up, traditional theories on industrial structure, represented by Clark's Law, certainly played a role in guiding economic development over a certain historical period. However, with in-depth social and economic development, its fundamental theoretical fallacies are gradually exposed. These theories can no longer provide appropriate guidance, and even worse, may lead economic development astray.

Notes

1. Angus Maddison, *A Bicentennial Review of World Economy*, trans. LI Dewei et al. (Beijing: Reform Press, 1997), 59, 76, 112, 134, 149, 157.

2. Kuznets calls the primary industry, secondary industry and tertiary industry as the agricultural sector, industrial sector and service sector respectively.

CHAPTER 3

A New Theoretical Paradigm

The traditional theoretical paradigm of industrial structure represented by Clark's Law was proposed long ago. Several Nobel Prize winners have proved the existence of this paradigm through their own studies. However, Kuznets, Chenery, and even Bell – who crossed research fields – focused on limited time periods between the 1960s and 70s. In reality, from the First Industrial Revolution to the present, changes in industrial structure are by no means a one-off process. Moreover, the share of the service sector rises as an inevitable result of economic growth. However, it represents neither the ultimate direction nor the indicator of economic development.

The crux of the matter is questioning the academic conscience of economists – should we adapt economic activity to theory, or bring theory closer to reality? Should we strive for economic prosperity, or yield to economic recession just because it accompanies a high share of the service sector? Should economics seek to maximize benefits under the rational allocation of resources, or follow the existing so-called law and give up the effort to pursue prosperity?

In view of these questions, a new theoretical paradigm is hereby proposed to address the defects of the traditional industrial structure.

Section 1   Theoretical Premises and Theoretical Logic

As noted above, in order to avoid the fallacies of conventional industrial structure theories, it is proposed that the relationship between industrial structure and economic growth should adhere to the basic premises and framework as follows: i) Measure economic development by economic growth rate; ii) Take into consideration international industrial structure; iii) Apply internationally recognized statistical standards to industrial classification; and iv) Change the indicator from labor force to GDP.

I. *Economic Growth Rate*

As previously mentioned, traditional theories on industrial structure presupposed "economic growth" as the core theoretical premise. In order to accurately analyze the relationship between industrial structure and economic growth, the author proposes a relative quantitative indicator that can reflect the scale of economic growth fluctuation – the economic growth rate is the main indicator defining economic development. Almost every country in the world shows long-term economic growth; the indicator of economic growth cannot reflect the relationship between industrial structure and economic growth, but economic growth rate can. Yet, since WWII countries across the world have successively chosen Keynesian theories to guide economic development. As new technologies continuously emerge, the world economy is characterized by long-term growth with short-term depressions as well as general growth with structural depression. Therefore, whether an economy grows or not can only be judged through an international comparison of economic growth rates in different economies.

In fact, when examining national economic growth, it is necessary to review long-term increases in population and per capita product in absolute terms, as well as relative increases in population and per capita product compared to other countries. Here, we presuppose economic growth in a relative sense, that is, we use the economic growth rate to examine the relationship between economic growth and industrial structure, and apply the dynamic theory of relativity to comparative research within and across countries. In this way, short- and mid-term fluctuations will not be rejected in the analysis of long-term trends.

II. Open Economy

Traditional research on industrial structure often negated the influence brought about by international economic cooperation. In fact, as the open economy developed greatly after WWII, the industrial structure of an open country or region became inseparable from the international economic cycle; the industrial structures of various countries formed a large supranational community-style industrial structure dependent on material production as a whole to drive the economic development of member states. Because national industries are only part of the global economy, the industrial structure may be dominated by a particular sector.

For example, some smaller countries such as Andorra and the Vatican survive on the service sector. However, without independent economic activities, their prosperity depends on the industrial sector of nations which they trade with. This is particularly important for countries that are highly open and dependent on the world economy, such as the United States. Production and consumption in the US, as the world's largest economy, are significantly influenced by overseas material production sectors. However, due to statistical data limitations, this overseas influence is set as a fixed value for reference only. In contrast, China has only been part of the world economic system for a short period; it is mostly involved in international cooperation through imports and exports, thus it is primarily subject to influence in this area.

III. *Industrial Classification Standards*

As mentioned earlier, the difference in industrial classification between traditional theories affects analysis. The fundamental divergence between the various classification standards concerns the categorization of transportation and electricity. In the early industrialization stage, electricity and other public utilities, transportation, and communication were basically created and operated to meet the needs of industry – their production was basically included in the production processes of industry. With the development of industrial society, and in particular with the rise of technological revolution after WWII, the economic growth of mass consumption became a major feature. However, public utilities, transportation and communication begin to break away from industry: they partly serve public consumption and partly services, such as commerce and finance, thereby indirectly serving mass consumption. Of course, they partly continue to perform their original function of serving industry, but this part is no longer so advantageous; meanwhile, electricity still maintains the characteristics of industrial production. It is mainly used by the industrial sector as a whole, although it also serves social consumption. Therefore, at this stage, electricity should be classified as part of the industrial sector, while transportation and communication should be classified as services.

Based on investigation across the above historical periods, from the perspective of development, we classify electricity as industry and transportation and communication as services. The new theoretical paradigm hereby proposed basically adopts the national statistical standards of China and the United States

Table 3.1 Comparison of Industrial Classification Methods

Division mode	Fischer	Clark	Kuznets	New Theoretical Paradigm
Primary industry	Agriculture, forestry, fishery and hunting	Agriculture, animal husbandry, fishery, forestry and hunting	Agricultural and aquatic products	Agriculture
Secondary industry	Mining, manufacturing, construction, power and gas and other public utilities	Mining, manufacturing, construction, public utilities and power	Mining, manufacturing, construction, power, transportation, post and telecommunications, communication and others	Mining, manufacturing, construction, water, power and gas and other public utilities
Tertiary industry	Public services such as commerce, finance and public administrative services such as science, education, culture, health and government	Commerce, transportation, administration, family services and other industries of immaterial production	Commerce, finance, real estate, individuals, enterprises, family services, professional services and government services	Transportation, post and telecommunications, commerce, finance, real estate, individuals, enterprises, family services, professional services and government services
Main differences with new theoretical paradigm	Transportation and communication belong to the secondary industry	Post and telecommunications and communication belong to the tertiary industry	Transportation, post and telecommunications and communication belong to the secondary industry, and water and gas belong to the tertiary industry	

Source: Compiled by the author based on relevant studies.

for industrial classification: more specifically, the primary sector includes agriculture, animal husbandry, forestry, fishing and hunting; the secondary sector includes mining, manufacturing, construction, and public utilities such as electricity and gas; and the tertiary sector includes transportation, postal services and telecommunications, communication, commerce, finance, real estate, personal, entrepreneurial and household services, special services, and government services.

The difference between the traditional and the proposed theoretical paradigm will not make our research less scientific or less capable to test traditional theories. Firstly, as the classification method we adopt is internationally accepted at present, our research falls in line with international practices. Secondly, we find that secondary sector development relates positively to GDP growth. Our research is convictive, because the secondary sector classified by our standard is even lower in absolute GDP value than the secondary sector by former researchers. A comparison of industrial classification methods is shown in Table 3.1.

IV. GDP as an Indicator of Industrial Structure

As mentioned earlier, Clark's Law used labor force as the indicator to examine changes in the distribution of labor among industries during economic development. The practice is contradictory to the selection of national income as the indicator instead.

For this reason, we propose using GDP as the indicator to examine changes in the share of each sector in the process of economic (or GDP) growth, so as to accurately grasp each sector's contribution, status, and impact on economic growth. As such, the relationship between industrial structure and economic growth can be made clearer.

Section 2   Industrial Structure and Economic Growth

It is necessary to clarify the following fundamental mechanisms in the evolution of industrial structure: i) The material production sector as the foundation of economic society; ii) The long-term trend of industrial development determined by its own mechanism; and iii) The mechanism of the effect of industrial structure on economic growth.

I. *Factors Determining the Fundamental Position of the Material Production Sector*

From the perspective of industrial structure, there are only two forms of economic society in the past, present and future: agriculture-centered and industry-centered. The society that centers on the service (tertiary) sector as described by Clark's Law will not exist.

An agricultural or industrial society refers to an economic society in which the agricultural or industrial sector plays a major role in driving economic development compared to other sectors. In terms of industrial structure, the agricultural or industrial sector takes the dominant position, the rise of whose share forms an inevitable causal relationship with economic growth. With the development of social productivity, a transition from an agricultural society to an industrial society is inevitable, but both societies center on material production. Material production has always been the foundation for the existence and development of social economy for the following reasons:

1. Needs are the fundamental force driving the evolution of industrial structure, all levels of which are based on material needs. As income increases, spiritual needs grow faster than material needs, but they still rest on the development of material means. Therefore, the center of economic society must be the material production sector, not the non-material production sector.

Industrial structure reflects the proportional relationship between industries in the national economy. This proportional relationship, in essence, is determined by the comprehensive needs of each economic sector for social consumption – the ultimate goal of social mass production. Needs (or wants) refer to human desires for material and spiritual life. They include not only the part that can be "afforded," that is, demand, but also the part that cannot be satisfied by social and economic conditions at the time.

On theories of needs, the most popular is Abraham Maslow's hierarchy of needs introduced in 1943, which specifies five levels: i) Physiological needs, that is, the need for survival; ii) The need for safety; iii) The need for belongingness & love; iv) The need for esteem; v) The need for self-actualization. These needs arise one after another. More specifically, need at a higher level arises once need at a lower level is satisfied, albeit partially. In this sense, needs are practically infinite. Moreover, a need is not eliminated by the arrival or development of need at a higher level. The needs of various levels are interdependent and overlapping. While high-level needs develop constantly, low-level needs hold on, but with smaller influence on economic behavior.

Since then, many theories of needs have emerged. In 1972, Alderfer compressed Maslow's five levels of needs into three categories – existence, relatedness and growth – referred to as the ERG model. He said that when needs in a category are frustrated, an individual will invest more effort in this category; when needs in a lower category are satisfied, an individual will invest more effort in the higher category; when needs in a higher category are frustrated, an individual will invest more effort in the lower category.

Meanwhile, Soviet scholars argued that social needs are dominant in human behavior, determining the direction of human thinking. Therefore, they proposed the hierarchy of social needs: the need for social and political activities at the top, followed in descending order by the need for domination, the need for communication, the need for success, the need for cognition, and the need for artistic beauty.

The author believes that as a unique attribute of human beings, needs should include not only personal desires, but also the desires generated by society as a whole. In other words, needs essentially contain the material and spiritual needs of individuals and groups at all levels. These depend on, promote and penetrate each other based on the common foundation of material needs.

Firstly, material needs ensure human survival and continuity. They represent the basic purpose and starting point for humans to engage in economic activities. Therefore, for much of early human society (which had very low social productivity), food was the first necessity and agriculture was upheld as the central economic sector.

Secondly, the expansion of material needs gave impetus to social productivity advancement. As the basic needs to ensure survival and continuity are gradually secured and even exceeded, people's needs will grow. The focus shifts from just food to food, clothing, and housing and further to clothing, housing, and transportation. All these require larger quantities and higher quality of material goods, as well as the advancement of social production and technology. In order to meet these ever-changing and growing material needs, industry overtakes agriculture to occupy the core position of economic society.

Finally, spiritual needs are also based on material products: as income increases, spiritual needs will grow faster than material needs. However, this does not mean that economic activities will deviate from material production, since spiritual needs rest on material products. For example, the appreciation of music depends on the manufacture and continuous innovation of musical instruments and audio equipment. Knowledge research and absorption requires more leisure time, which can be realized by improving the labor productivity of material production and saving labor time.

2. Even if human society surpasses the commodity economy and develops into a communist society, mankind still cannot shake off reliance on material products.

The advancement of material production, especially the development of the industrial sector, "will provide society with enough products to meet the needs of all the members."[1] At this point, the commodity economy will eventually be replaced by the product economy – where each takes what they need. Industries that exist only in the commodity economy along with commodity exchange and currency, such as commerce, finance, and real estate, and government services such as state management and national defense, will all wither away. The vast majority of them fall to services. To summarize, after entering the product economy, most industries in the service sector will no longer exist, let alone dominate the economy and society.

3. In the commodity economy stage, the service sector can neither drive forward the economy, nor become its focal point.

Firstly, the service sector stems from material production and provides services for the material production process. In this regard, we cannot turn the cart before the horse. As Karl Marx said, "The conclusion which follows from this is, not that production, distribution, exchange and consumption are identical, but that they are links of a single whole – different aspects of one unit. Production is the decisive phase, both with regard to its contradictory aspects and with to other phases. The process always starts afresh with production. That exchange and consumption cannot be the decisive elements is obvious; and the same applies to distribution in the sense of distribution of products."[2] Hence, commerce in the service sector exists only to fulfill the intermediary role in the circulation of industrial capital; finance to solve difficulties in raising industrial capital and in completing the means of payment; and transportation to connect the various intermediary points of material products in the process of production, distribution, exchange and consumption. Services (in the narrow sense) in the fields of individuals, households, enterprises and governments are even more subordinate to the entire material production process. Moreover, from a quantitative perspective, the share of services is determined by material production. "A distinct mode of production thus determines the specific mode of consumption, distribution, exchange and the specific relations of these different phases."[3] Essentially, the service sector should not develop in excess of production needs. If so, unneeded services would not be conducive to economic development, but harmful to a healthy society. Hence, from the objective law of economic and social operation, it is absurd for the service sector to dominate the economy.

Secondly, the service sector takes a dominant position in some countries, however this is based on the development of material production in other nations; it is by no means representative of a circular economy. Historically, many countries suffered due to an overemphasis on services at the expense of material production – for example in the 16th century the Netherlands held a relatively supreme position due to maritime trade and plunder, however it later lost this maritime hegemony to Britain. Britain had developed greatly from the Industrial Revolution, yet it followed the same path as the Netherlands after becoming the world's premier factory and center of economic power. It neglected its own innovation and development in favor of colonial trade, eventually being surpassed by the United States as the world's leading economy.

Finally, practice has proved that expanding services beyond the needs of material production will not only fail to drive economic growth, but also lead to long-term economic depression and recession. The many cycles of agricultural society in China are precise consequences of commercial agriculture erosion. The modern British decline, the US long-term slump after the late 1960s, and Japan's economic slowdown and debt crisis after the 1970s are all associated with service sector growth that exceeded or even deviated from the needs of industry. The industrial structure has statistically shown that services have occupied a dominant share for a long time. People are misled into believing the arrival of a service-centered society. But in essence, this displays the relative decline of industry as the driving force of economic growth, resulting in a long-term economic depression.

II. Mechanism for Determining the Long-term Trend of Industrial Development

Judging from the path of economic and social development so far, industrial development has shown its own long-term trends. In an agricultural society, agriculture plays a central role in the industrial structure, having developed gradually over a long time period. As agricultural development and commercialization catalyzed industrialization, the economic center shifted from agriculture to industry. In such a society, agriculture tends to exhibit a long-term downward trend, while the service sector shows a wave-like pattern of development in accordance with industry.

1. The long-term decline of agricultural share is determined by its technology development mechanism and consumption characteristics.

Firstly, in terms of demand and consumption structure, agricultural products are the most basic material necessities of life. In a period when agricultural productivity was still underdeveloped, these essential needs must be satisfied as much as possible in order to ensure social stability. Therefore, agriculture must be put at the helm. Agricultural development inevitably leads to commercialization, however, before agricultural labor productivity can break completely free from the shackles of satisfying essential needs, commercialization will eventually impair agricultural production itself. Consequently, agriculture is subject to erosion by commerce and plunged into depression from prosperity. Thus, governments and rulers resort to polices the reinstate agriculture at the economic center – this creates a long-term pattern of agricultural fluctuation.

With the advancement of agricultural technology, agricultural surplus increases, propelling commercialization and industrialization and thus reducing the agricultural share. In this respect, German statistician L. E. Engel argued powerfully.[4] As income increases, demand for agricultural products lags relatively behind the demand for industrial and service products, leading

Table 3.2 International Comparison of Labor Productivity between the
Three Sectors (Average Values for 1948–1954)

Per capita national income	National income	Labor productivity and its comparison		
		A (Primary industry)	B (Secondary and tertiary industry)	A/B
1	7	0.86	1.03	0.86
2	6	0.60	1.19	0.52
3	6	0.69	1.15	0.62
4	5	0.48	2.02	0.27
5	5	0.61	1.48	0.42
6	7	0.69	1.72	0.45
7	4	0.67	2.74	0.31

Source: Simon Kuznets, "Quantitative Aspects of The Economic Growth of Nations: II Industrial Distribution of National Product and Labor Force," *Economic Development and Cultural Change* 5, no. 4 (1957): 1–111.

to a decrease of national income in agriculture and an increase in other industrial sectors. This creates price gaps between agricultural products and industrial products & social services, allowing for higher added value, derived from higher prices, of industrial products and social services. As a result, agricultural income falls even further and labor continues to flow to other sectors. Table 3.2 shows the international comparison of labor productivity between the three sectors in the post-war period.

Secondly, the income elasticity of agricultural products is low. However, this should be viewed historically. In an agricultural society, the most basic needs of life should also be urgently met. Due to low labor productivity, income growth was to a large extent associated with the increase in agricultural products; the income elasticity of agriculture was still relatively high. After entering the industrial stage, increases in labor productivity and income made it easier to meet these basic needs – consumption focus shifted to industrial products.

Thirdly, it is much more difficult to make technological progress in agriculture than in industry. Moreover, due to the intrinsic characteristics of agricultural production, agricultural investment is prone to "diminishing returns." This, combined with the low income elasticity of agricultural demand and high income elasticity of industrial demand, will inevitably reduce the relative share of agriculture in national income.

Fourthly, as agriculture labor productivity increases, coupled with land limitation and low income elasticity, labor released by agriculture will inevitably flow into other industries. Kuznets divided 40 countries into seven groups according to per capita national income. He investigated the comparative labor productivity of the primary, secondary and tertiary industries from 1948 to 1954, finding that the poorer the country, the larger the comparative labor productivity gap between the primary industry and the secondary & tertiary industries. Moreover, most underdeveloped countries are agricultural with a large proportion of agricultural labor; while developed countries are mostly industrial with a small proportion of agricultural labor.

Finally, as a result of commercialization and industrialization, some of the cottage industries that were originally affiliated with the agricultural sector are reclassified to the industrial sector through specialized division of labor, such as food processing, cotton spinning, and farm tool manufacturing. This further shows up as a statistical decline in agricultural share.

2. The rapid increase in the share of industry is closely related to its technical features and consumer market characteristics.

Firstly, because of low agricultural productivity in agrarian societies, production must meet the basic needs (as much as possible) for agricultural products. With the improvement of labor productivity and the continuous expansion of material and spiritual needs, industrial products gradually rise to dominate the demand and consumption structures. It is the continuous extension of social needs that supports the continuous increase of the industrial share.

Secondly, the income elasticity of industrial products is high. As income increases, spiritual consumption growth will outpace material consumption growth. Therefore, with national income increases, industry will receive more support than agriculture and services, which stimulate its development.

Thirdly, the industrialization of agriculture, the advancement of industrial technology, and the rise of emerging industries have continuously strengthened the industrial sector in both quality and quantity. Industries that originally fell to agriculture, such as food processing and textiles, have transferred to and enriched the industrial sector. The industrialization of agricultural production methods, such as the popularization of agricultural machinery and the widespread application of chemical fertilizers, has also fueled industrial expansion. More importantly, propelled by technological revolution, new industries have continuously emerged and production efficiency has increased rapidly within industry, directly creating this sector's growth trend.

Fourth, compared with agriculture and services, rapid technological progress and high labor productivity enable industry to create national wealth more efficiently. Driven by technological advance, its share in the national economy grows faster, exhibiting a relatively upward trend.

Finally, the wave-like development of industry in an industrial society is the inevitable result of the cyclical nature of technological revolution. Catalyzed by technological revolution, the industrial sector continues to create new products to meet market needs. As the market becomes saturated with industrial technology, industrial production tends to contract, as does its share in the national economy. In order to overcome deficiencies of the old technological system, a new round of technological revolution emerges. Driven by this, the share of industry rises once again before technology matures and ages. Such cyclical changes characterize the undulating development of industry.

In a capitalist system, wave-like development is manifested as follows: through many small economic cycles, the share of industry is raised within the range allowed by the existing technological system. Simultaneously, as production expands asynchronously with demand of affordability, economic contradictions accumulate until the outbreak of a large-scale economic crisis. Such crises result in much bankruptcy and more intense market competition. In face of an industrial slowdown, industry is forced to leverage technological revolution to escape trouble.

The new technological revolution enables the economy to recover from the crisis and head for another boom.

3. The service sector is not the decisive force, though its share rises faster than agriculture.

Firstly, compared with agriculture, its income elasticity is high: as income increases, the demand for services grows faster than the demand for agriculture. In addition, services are subordinate to the material production sector, especially industry. It will expand with the growth of this. Therefore, its relative weight in national income will rise accordingly.

Secondly, compared with industry, the service sector is difficult to form a monopoly in but easy to absorb labor, which also contributes to the increase of its employment share. Judging from the situation of several developed countries in Europe and America from the early 20th century to the 1960s, the labor separated from agriculture was mainly absorbed by services. Because of relatively easy access to labor and capital, competition within many industries in the service sector is fierce, making monopoly unlikely. Consequently, services as an intangible commodity are dwarfed by industrial products as tangible commodities in terms of added value.

Nevertheless, the capacity of services to absorb employment also tends to gradually decline with technological progress. Advanced technology and automated office equipment reduce the labor demand of services by raising labor productivity. For example, the application of computer networks increases the pressure on operating costs while greatly improving the office efficiency of industries such as commerce and finance. According to a study from the Boston Consulting Group in 2018 (*Replacement or Liberation: The Impact of Artificial Intelligence on the Financial Labor Market*), it is forecast by that by 2027, China's financial industry will have 9.93 million employees – a cut of 2.3 million jobs due to artificial intelligence.

Thirdly, as mentioned earlier, the service sector provides services based on material carriers, and serves the material production sector directly or indirectly. Though rapid, the growth of its share is accompanied by the growth of the material production sector (i.e., the agricultural sector in an agricultural society, and the industrial sector in an industrial society).

Finally, the service sector develops wave-on-wave with fluctuations in the industrial sector. When industry is thriving, the service sector develops accordingly, but at a slower pace, so its share shows a relative decline. When industry falls to depression with technology maturity and aging, the service sector continues to develop for a while due to material production inertia and consumption patterns. Among them, commerce, finance, education and state agencies are less threatened by aging technology because their services have constituted a relatively fixed part of production and life. Some service industries, such as securities, banking, futures, and real estate, have even seen self-circulation and malignant expansion. Therefore, services maintain a better condition than industry, which is embodied in a relative increase in the service share. In short, the service sector share fluctuates alternately with the industrial sector in the long run.

III. Effect of Industrial Structure on Economic Growth

The growth of the material production sector is the fundamental force driving national economic development. In an economic boom, the proportion of material production rises as its growth outpaces that of other sectors.

First of all, spiritual needs must rest on material products. Industrial products (agricultural products) as the most important consumer products in an industrial society (agricultural society) can, to the maximum extent, satisfy material and spiritual needs. It is precisely on this foundation that material production becomes the fundamental driving force for economic development. Hence, the industrial sector (agricultural sector) is the leading sector of industrial society (agricultural society).

Secondly, regardless of historical stages, social productivity is enabled by the expansion and optimization of production objects, and the invention and precision of production tools as well as the improvement of labor's understanding of the physical world. Thus, only with improvements in material production can technological advances gradually promote social value growth. As the material carrier of technology, the material production sector will naturally become the driving force of social progress.

Finally, practice has proved that during the industrial boom (agricultural society), the industrial sector (agricultural sector) achieved faster development relative to other sectors, and thus saw its economic share grow. In China, previous prosperity derived from agricultural society came after stable agricultural production development. Among developed countries, Japan and the United States experienced rapid development of the entire economy based on rapid industrial growth. A concrete manifestation of this is the continuous increase in industrial share of the national economy.

Section 3 New Conclusions and Related Theoretical Issues

Although we can prove that material production is the fundamental force, some economists still regard the rising share of the tertiary industry in some developed countries as an inevitable trend of social development. They fail to see, dialectically, that such a rise is closely associated with economic recession, and forget the ultimate goal of theoretical economic research.

I. New Conclusions

Based on the theoretical analysis above and the experiences of major industrial countries, emerging industrial countries in Asia, and China, new conclusions can be made about the evolution of industrial structure and its relationship with economic growth.

First, the transformation of industrial structure is not a one-off process in which each sector takes a turn to occupy the largest share; rather, it's a process in which the primary industry share declines in the long run, while the secondary and tertiary industry sectors both go through several trough-peak-trough cycles. This has been proved by the practices of many countries.

Second, after an economy begins industrialization, secondary industry will gradually become the driving force. In the long run, when this share rises or maintains a high level, economic growth quickens or maintains its high speed. Contrarily, when the share of the tertiary industry grows or remains high, economic growth slows or the economy falls into recession or crisis. In fact, secondary industry cycles usually go step-by-step with industrial revolution cycles, whereas tertiary industry is the opposite. This shows that rapid secondary industry development driven by technological progress positively correlates with changes in economic growth; quantitative analysis will be introduced to prove these arguments.

Third, based on aforementioned conclusions of international industrial structure, we are still in a period when secondary industry plays the decisive role in economic growth, that is, we are still in an industrial society. Although the share of the tertiary industry in the US is comparatively high, it cannot change the fact that economic growth is driven by the secondary industry. It can only underline how the tertiary sector is built on the global industrial system and takes a relatively high-end position. To date, no country has gone beyond industrial society and entered the so-called post-industrial society.

II. Understanding the Tertiary Share Increase

The tertiary industry share is indeed increasing in some economically developed and emerging industrial countries. Judging from objective reality, since these countries are in a relatively advanced position, many people believe the continuous increase in the tertiary industry signals that an economy has reached a developed stage; it represents an inevitable trend of economic development. Such increases, therefore, prove the tertiary industry will occupy the central position of national economy. In our opinion, this view is misled by the advantages of developed countries in the static status quo. It should be noted that the continuous rise in tertiary industry share is accompanied by the deceleration of economic growth. If furthered, this change will result in economic crisis and long-term depression. There are many examples in this regard.

In addition, the influence of Kant's philosophy – that what is real is reasonable – cannot be ignored. This philosophy has value when used to examine the objective physical world, but it is not applicable to the study of human behavior integrating world outlooks and values, including economic behavior. As spiritual and material civilizations are being created with social development, the darker side of this becomes more exposed: the increasing social force of capital, uncurbed corruption, increasing crime, etc. These phenomena are real, but by no means reasonable. On this account, the aforementioned view of certain economists is completely oblivious to the nature of humans as higher animals.

III. About the Significance of Economics

Some economists uphold the notion that an increase in the tertiary sector is justified by Kant's philosophy. This view reminds us that economics itself has lost direction. It has been dedicated to examining the so-called economic phenomena that have been "alienated," while ignoring world outlooks and values that human beings should have. As noted earlier, Western theories on industrial structure are not flawless in theoretical premises, research methods, conclusions, and theoretical logic.

In terms of motivation, the fundamental cause of deficiencies is that economics does not study the generation mechanism of economic behavior from a human perspective, but seeks precise reasoning and proof based on the trajectory of formed economic behavior. The premises are unable to generalize all aspects of economy and society, and can only cover some aspects of the static situation rather than the dynamic process. To this end, the only approach uses hypothesis instead of reality. At the same time, human society is constantly progressing, and economic behavior is gradually changing. The study of external and operable economic phenomena that have been "alienated" fails to take human motivation of economic behavior into account. Consequently, it can only follow older theories, and claim to predict the future by relying on inert economic behavior. This negative feature of economics is also extremely inconsistent with the positive feature of economic behavior.

However, as far as the research activities of natural and social sciences are concerned, the internal mechanism of things is perceived only based on real phenomena, and then perceptions are raised based on iterative in-depth studies, so as to be recognized as a relative truth in a certain historical stage. Western economics, as a subject that focuses on social and economic activities, is certainly no exception. Since economic behavior constantly changes with peoples' comprehension of the law of economic activity and their needs as individuals and groups, economic conclusions are unavoidably subject to time limitations. That being so, the significance of economics exists only in such a form: to provide a summary and prediction of the existence and development of the modes of economic thinking through research of human needs, and to propose economic goals that should be achieved in a future timeframe along with corresponding plans of action; rather than to conclude, based on past economic phenomena, that some result is inevitable in the future, on the assumption that human society is no longer progressing.

In terms of purpose, the study of economic development over a time period should not be aimed at explaining the internal mechanism based on its past trajectory. Instead, the study should, facing the future, guide subsequent social and individual economic activities. This involves questioning whether the conclusions derived from economics are purely factual descriptions or explanations with moral judgments. The answer to this question determines whether economics can guide future economic activities.

In this regard, David Hume raised the proposition that "'ought' cannot be inferred from 'is'" in his work *A Treatise of Human Nature*. This proposition is aptly called Hume's Guillotine due to the strict distinction between moral and evaluative fields. By this logical distinction, economics, if "summarizing the objective facts" as it has always stressed, cannot be used to guide human behavior, whose fundamental characteristic lies in initiative. It can only be appreciated as an achievement completed by human beings, like an exquisite exhibit in an art museum. But as mentioned earlier, the significance of economics is to guide economic activities. The will of human society has never been to repeat the past but to create the future. For this reason, economics must abandon the old habit of only studying economic phenomena in order to advertise "objectivity," and must embrace the world of "subjective initiative."

In summary, the ultimate goal of economics is to guide economic behavior to satisfy the needs of individuals and groups at all levels. Therefore, study must start from the law of economic behavior of human society. Economics stemmed from this should not only trace the past, but also serve the future to meet the ever-changing needs of mankind.

Notes

1. Frederick Engels, *The Principle of Communism*, vol. 1, *Karl Marx Frederick Engels Collected Works* (Beijing: People's Publishing House, 1972), 222.

2. Karl Marx, *A Contribution to the Critique of Political Economy (Introduction)*, vol. 2, *Karl Marx Frederick Engels Collected Works* (Beijing: People's Publishing House, 1972), 102.

3. Ibid.

4. In his paper "The Production and Consumption of the Kingdom of Saxony," Engel points out that in the low-income countries, the proportion of food costs in household expenditures is higher. This assertion is later called Engel's Law. The percentage of food costs in total household expenditure is called Engel's Coefficient.

CHAPTER 4

Evidence from Reality: Agricultural Society

Agricultural society refers to a society in which agriculture plays the leading role in economic development relative to other sectors, such as handicraft and commerce. Agriculture dominates the industrial structure correspondingly. The rise in agricultural share inevitably has a causal influence on economic growth. At this stage the following trends occur: agriculture advances wave-on-wave while maintaining a dominant position; handicraft develops slowly for a long time; and commerce fluctuates with agriculture.

Here, China and Japan are taken as examples to examine this evolution. China was most prosperous as an agricultural society, reaching the pinnacle of the world; thus, it can be deemed a model agricultural society. Moreover, China has been at this stage for up to thousands of years. China reached this peak during the Han, Tang, Ming, and Qing dynasties. It provides the best material for investigating long-term trends, volatility, and the industrial cycle.

In this regard, Japan was far less prosperous than China, but considering it a typical one-cycle agricultural society, the investigation also has significance. In addition, Japan went through a rapid industrialization process and developed by leaps and bounds, adding to its value as a case-study. Meanwhile, European agricultural society was mostly characterized by animal husbandry. Agricultural production progress was not as clear and diversified as that of China, and the development of animal husbandry was not essential to industrialization. To be specific, industrialization in Europe was intimately connected to its colonization and plunder across the globe, thus it does not serve as a typical example when observing agricultural trends in economics.

Section 1   Evolution of Industrial Structure

I.   *Agriculture as the Economic Center*
Through analysis in this chapter, it can be shown that economies always progresses upward. However, this process is not smooth – it is embodied in the generation, development, evolution and transfer of the central sector. It stems from contradictions between productive forces, production relations, and material and spiritual needs in a certain historical period, and reflects the

quantitative and qualitative changes in industrial technology. It is a combined result of inevitability and contingency in social development.

Productive forces and material and spiritual needs are constantly developing. Since the social division of labor occurred, most basic material needs have been met. In this sense, after the separation of handicrafts from agriculture, social needs demanded the continued development of agriculture on the one hand and the further expansion of the handicraft industry on the other hand – essentially a shift from the economic center to handicrafts. This tendency became apparent when agricultural production reached a relatively stable state. However, agricultural productivity was still very low. It could only meet most basic material needs when there were no natural or man-made disasters. For this reason, production relations interfered in the process placed agriculture at the center.

In some economies, however, there were fewer accidental factors such as natural and man-made disasters; yet agricultural productivity was not high enough to support large-scale commercialization and industrialization. Agricultural develop-ment was, relatively speaking, less sporadic. It was steady on the whole and despite fluctuations usually showed an upward trend. Japan is representative of such countries. No matter whether these fluctuations were prominent or not, agriculture maintained the dominant economic position, so long as agricultural productivity could effectively overcome natural conditions and human factors, and meet basic material needs. Of course, blows to agricultural production and the subsequent short term declines were unavoidable. However, such declines only resulted from external factors in the development process. It does not mean the central sector had shifted from agriculture to commerce or handicraft. This is eloquently proved by China's history.

II. *Long-term Solidification of Chinese Agriculture*

Chinese agricultural society has been through two cycles. In the first, an agriculture-based economic system was established in the Zhou Dynasty (1046–771 BC) and reformed in the Qin Dynasty (221–206 BC). Following prosperity in the Han Dynasty, this system declined in the Three Kingdoms and the Jin Dynasty, and was abolished in the Southern and Northern Dynasties.

In the second cycle, the agriculture-based economic system was restored during Northern Wei and began to thrive in the Sui and Tang dynasties; later, commercialization strengthened in the middle and late Ming Dynasty. However, during the Qing Dynasty (1644–1912), as the social system regressed, the economy was suppressed; agriculture did not prosper, while commerce was restrained. For thousands of years, China was governed by an agricultural-based system that put commerce last. The dominance of agriculture did not change, although there were certain periods when commerce was not restrained. The trend of commercialization was not necessarily caused by the development of production, but resulted from social production breaking through feudal resistance. In general, the commercialization of the Chinese economy was slow, repetitive, and prolonged for many reasons.

First, dynasties changed frequently and wars broke out continuously. Typically, less advanced tribal groups conquered more advanced groups by means of force, and the more developed societies returned to more basic ways of living. As a result, the change of dynasties was effectively a cycle of fall and rise, with little economic progress.

These less-advanced groups were rarely well versed in agricultural affairs. When the Han people regained control of the country, the economy was depressed due to long-term wars and chaos. For this reason, each newly established dynasty drew on the system of the previous dynasty and aimed to restore its prosperity; mindset and behavior pattern were fixed by following the old routine.

Third, the long-standing policy of "emphasizing agriculture and restraining industry & commerce" was firmly encouraged and ultimately restricted industry development. From the perspective of market factors, residents were largely self-sufficient, resulting in a narrow market – feudal officials and aristocracies constituted the main consumers; their large consumption would lessen the government treasury and put the country in danger. The economy was bound to collapse after reaching its zenith. From the perspective of capital, industry and commerce often turned to land rent and usury due to profit exploitation and social turmoil. There was a lack of long-term business goals and capital reinvestments. From a technological perspective, handicraftsmen had respective skills. Whenever there was war, craftsmen became a target contested by the military and the authorities; they were often forced to accompany the military and perform as ordered. If they won, they would be slaughtered to avoid future troubles. If they lost, they would be killed to prevent employment by others. In the end, handcraft skills were lost with the death of handicraftsmen. In addition, due to conservative and foolish thinking, the Four Great Inventions (papermaking, gunpowder, printing, and the compass) were not well used. From a human perspective, the inheritance of occupations (gentry scholars, peasants, craftsmen, and merchants) from generation to generation prevented the expansion of commerce and industry to some extent. He who excelled in study could follow an official career: this long-standing policy turned the possibility of promoting technological progress into the reality of propagating reading and writing mechanically. Consequently, there were few technical innovators emerging over thousands of years.

Eventually, with the failure of the Opium War and a series of wars in self-defense, the Qing Dynasty was forced to initiate the Westernization Movement – the first step in China's industrialization efforts.

III. *Learner – Japan*

Japanese feudal society was largely influenced by China, which it imported technology and its social system from; thus it gained a very similar social nature to China, however, the two countries differed in other ways.

First, wars and dynastic changes in Japan were not as frequent as in China. More importantly, as a one-nation maritime island, Japan was able to repel potential foreign aggressors and occupation at a time when technology was underdeveloped. Genghis Khan once attacked, but failed to cross the seas successfully. Thus, the socio-economic system remained relatively unchanged over a long period, with basic socio-economic trends largely free from external impacts.

Second, Japan did not stick to its old social system to restore previous prosperity, but introduced China's more advanced social system instead. Ultimately, its behavior was not incompatible with innovation and was less rigid than China's.

In other aspects – an emphasis on agriculture ahead of industry and commerce, the social hierarchy, and imperial examinations – were all coped from China, as well as Confucianism, Taoism, and Buddhism. In general, Japan lagged behind China up to the late 19th century in terms of social and economic development. The key to the subsequent economic take-off and expansion lies in the different internal and external preconditions between China and Japan in the initial industrialization stage.

Looking back at agrarian society, China and Japan witnessed a very similar industrial structure evolution: agriculture was central to the economy, commerce rose and fell with agriculture, and handicrafts were always relegated to a peripheral position. Yet, in terms of cycles the two nations had very different experiences. China went through four main cycles (with smaller cycles formed at the changing of dynasty), exerting considerable destruction upon the system's development. In contrast, Japan experienced only one main cycle – from the Taika Reforms era (645 AD) to the Meiji Restoration (1868).

However, there are differences in specific cycles. In each one, small cycles were formed with the replacement of dynasties, and exerted considerable destruction in social and economic aspects, whereas Japan experienced one cycle only. Clearly, restraining commerce was common in both societies. China's slow and interrupted transition from an agricultural to an industrial society is mainly attributed to more serious ideological constraints and the enslavement of much handicraft in feudal society. In comparison, the constraint on ideas was weaker in Japan.

Section 2   Evidence from China

I.   *Four Historical Stages*

China has a long history of agriculture with many fluctuations. In terms of industrial structure, there were four historical stages:

1. From the formation of industry to non-restraints on commerce & industry at the end of the Eastern Zhou Dynasty and the Warring States Period. Due to data constraints, it is unknown exactly when industry formed and division of labor began in China. According to archaeological results, it is very likely that agriculture developed independently. Evidence includes remains of rice found 9,000 years ago in the Yangtze River Basin; remains of ancient cultivated rice from 10,000 years ago in Daoxian County, Hunan; and garden-style agricultural relics in South China where root crops and fruit trees were planted around 10,000 years ago. It can be inferred that Chinese agriculture emerged in the early Neolithic Age (12,000–9,000 years ago).

The Caoxie Mountain Ruins along the Yangtze suggest that China had well-developed paddy fields around 6000 years ago, whilst industry and commerce also existed before the Yin-Shang Dynasty. In the Zhou era, handicrafts and commerce were still underdeveloped and largely prohibited, but occasionally encouraged by feudal lords. At the end of the Warring States Period, agriculture was unable to bear the levies and exploitation incurred by frequent wars and the erosion of industry & commerce; after this period, commerce & industry were less restrained.

2. The agriculture-centric stage occurred from reforms of Shang Yang in 350 BC to the middle of the Southern and Northern Dynasties in the 5th century. In the last years of the Warring States era, Shang Yang proposed supporting agriculture and restraining commerce; this policy not only laid the foundation for Qin's annexation of the six countries, but also created a successful model for subsequent dynasties. Consequently, agriculture developed tremendously under institutional incentives. But later, it was eroded by industry & commerce, and impacted by wars. Northern agriculture was even hit by foreign nomadic culture, and compared with the Central Plains, the southern region lagged far behind in agricultural production. In the Northern and Southern Dynasties, agriculture was on the verge of collapse, catalyzing industrial structure adjustment by institutional means.

3. During Taihe's reign in the Northern Wei Dynasty (485 AD), the equal-field (land equalization) system was introduced, rebuilding an agriculture-centered economic system. This was maintained in the following dynasties till the late Tang era, when

the private ownership of land became established. As the tax system had always centered on agriculture, this system continued until the Song Dynasty (960 AD). However, agriculture and industry & commerce did not prosper until the Tang and Song dynasties: agriculture was eroded by this once again at the end of Northern Song (1127), and hit by nomadic cultures from the north and west as well as attacked by foreign powers in later dynasties.

4. Agricultural commercialization during the Ming Dynasty. Owing to land reclamation incentives, the primary economic position of agriculture was restored in the mid-to-late 14th century. Later, industry & commerce were encouraged without compromising agriculture. In the ten years from the Jiaqing to the Chongzhen era (1531–1637), the Single Whip Reform was implemented, which allowed tax to be imposed on property instead of labor and collected in kind instead of in cash. This fiscal law stimulated the commodity economy, creating an opportunity for agricultural commercialization. However, agricultural production was undermined by increasing occupation of cropland by the imperial house and their courtiers and eunuchs. As the exploitation for military payments intensified to cope with the Jurchen people and Li Chuang's uprising army, agriculture eventually collapsed. China again fell into relative chaos.

In the Qing Dynasty, tax revenue encompassed labor corvee, tax in kind, and tax in money – more than half of which was sourced from tax in kind. The economic system was accordingly disposed towards agriculture and not commerce. Out of fear of the increasingly prosperous Han, the Qing government implemented even more acute policies to boost agriculture and restrain commerce, including a ban on maritime trade, which essentially hindered both commerce and agriculture. As a result, China missed a great opportunity to promote agricultural commercialization and industrialization. Only once China had been defeated by foreign powers, did the nation move in this direction.

To sum up, the aforementioned stages cover agricultural development, the subsequent boom of commerce and handicrafts that gradually threaten agriculture, resulting in social turmoil and national decline, and eventually the collapse of agriculture and decline of commerce. They manifest in the long rise-and-fall cycles of Chinese agricultural society. The evolution of industrial structure showed two obvious characteristics: i) Agriculture occupied a central position and its prosperity coincided with economic growth; and ii) Agriculture and commerce developed in a wave-like, cyclical manner with alternate fluctuations, while handicrafts progressed slowly in the long run. Below is an overview of the development process of the three sectors.

II. The Ups and Downs of Agriculture

Agriculture in China mostly took a path of undulating progress. There were four peak production periods in more than 3,000 years from the Yin-Shang Dynasty to the late Qing Dynasty.

The first peak was during the Warring States Period in Eastern Zhou. By the Spring and Autumn Period, ploughing and irrigation had already appeared. After entering the Warring States era, the iron plough became popular; cattle farming was introduced; and human, animal, and green manure were used. Simultaneously, water irrigation was also developed, and water conservancy (water projects) and gardening were separated from agriculture.

The second peak occurred during the Han Dynasty. First of all, there were great advances in farming tools and technologies which significantly increased labor efficiency in ploughing and planting, land utilization, and grain yields. In addition, water conservancy projects made headway, though frequent floods in Eastern Han brought severe blows to agricultural production.

The third peak covered the Tang and Song dynasties (608–1270). In the Tang, water irrigation developed continuously while no special progress was made in farming tools; sericulture and tea production began to rise notably. From the Song to the Yuan era, agricultural progress mainly manifested in three aspects: i) A variety of methods were used in the south to transform lakes to croplands, which enlarged farmland areas and promoted water conservancy; ii) In terms of irrigation equipment, man-powered waterwheels and Chinese water-powered noria became quite popular, while well water irrigation methods were also improved in the north; and iii) The cotton industry was advanced.

The fourth peak period lasted from the mid-Ming Dynasty to the mid-Qing Dynasty. In the Ming era, farming and irrigation methods evolved constantly: cotton planting was gradually expanded and practiced throughout and seed selection technology was also improved. Agricultural progress in the Qing (1644–1912) manifested in these aspects: i) Deep plowing, seed selection, multiple cropping, and fertilization technologies were developed; ii) Intensive management was promoted against the background of a population surge; iii) The introduction and promotion of new grains such as sorghum, corn, and sweet potato effectively alleviated the tension of land use; and iv) Cash crops such as cotton and linen also gained prominence.

In general, these four peak periods of agriculture brought prosperity to the entire economy and society, accordingly, demonstrating the characteristics of an agriculture-centered system.

III. Long-term Slow Handicraft Development

Handicraft in Chinese agricultural society made continuous progress in technology and division of labor. However, in industrial structure, it displayed a long-term slow development trend.

In the Zhou Dynasty, handicrafts become independent from agriculture with a highly specialized division of labor, among which smelting reached a considerable level. Iron farming tools were developed in the Spring and Autumn Period, while metallurgy made great progress and ironware was gradually applied during the Warring States Period. In the Han Dynasty, the division of labor in handicrafts was more refined. There was craft pottery, bronze ware and lacquerware. In addition, weaving was developed continuously and paper rose to prominence. Handicraft development after the Tang and Song dynasties most notably manifested in the separation of weaving from farming households, as well as in the highly developed porcelain industry.

Meanwhile, cotton was introduced in the Three Kingdoms Period. Cotton weaving became independent in the Yuan and Ming Dynasties and the dyeing industry developed accordingly. The abolition of a craftsman registration system in the Qing era facilitated, to a certain degree, handicraft commercialization. In addition, government-run handicraft workshops in the Ming and Qing dynasties, which exclusively used hired labor and purchased materials at "current prices," also contributed to the commodity economy. The Qing government initially imposed extremely strict measures on the scale of textile workshops: 100 at most. As the ban was lifted during the Kangxi era, the number of textile workshops increased to 500. Commercial capital was channeled to weaving, and gradually transformed into industrial capital.

The porcelain industry made strides in the Sui and Tang dynasties, and there were many famous kilns in the Song era. After the Ming period, many famous northern kilns were ravaged and thereafter Jingdezhen became the center of porcelain. In terms of technology, potter wheels, glazing by sufflation, and firing kilns were invented in this period. With the further development of porcelain-making technology, mass production was enabled in the early and mid-Qing era. In the late Qing, the division of labor became more refined, but concurrent operations were not allowed, resulting in small and scattered operations. This slowed the formation of the handicraft workshop system. Besides, considerable advances and spurts of capitalism were also seen in printing, iron smelting, tea, tobacco, wine, oil, sugar, copper, coal, salt and shipping industries.

IV.   Alternate Fluctuations of Commerce and Industry

Typically, commerce progressed gradually with agricultural development, then reached a climax while agriculture declined, and subsequently fell into disregard under the influence of social turmoil and war.

Commerce gradually became independent in the late Spring and Autumn Period, and began to flourish in the Warring States era. On the one hand, great progress in agriculture and handicrafts increased the surplus products available for exchange. On the other hand, the tributes paid on trade were no longer effective in the Warring States Period. Other contributive factors include market expansion with urbanization, the implantation of a gold standard during the Warring States, and coinage power in the hands of merchants.

In the Qin and Han dynasties, development of commerce was maintained due to four main reasons: first, pass and ferry checkpoints were all removed after national reunification in the Qin Dynasty, creating good logistical conditions. Second, noticing the stable development of agriculture, Empress Xiaohui Zhang relaxed commerce laws. Third, a unified measurement system was established in the Han Dynasty, enabling strict management. Fourth, the admission of merchants into government bodies not only attracted the largest consumer class, but also suppressed small merchants and civilians. At the same time, officials engaged in commerce themselves and a market was even formed within the army.

In the Tang Dynasty, with the restoration of agriculture and handicrafts, and the development of transportation, commerce management was gradually relaxed. Noble landlords and government officials took to business, promoting commercial development. Simultaneously, the earliest check and exchange systems were established.

In the Song Dynasty, commerce experienced great ups and downs due to the improvement of water transportation, the transfer of political centers, and fluctuations in agriculture and handicraft. As the measurement system was basically abolished in the mid-Northern Song era, transactions were not restricted to urban areas and could be carried out day and night. Regarding foreign maritime trade, it made considerable profits as early as the Five Dynasties. By following this practice, the Song pursued this development.

In the Ming Dynasty, the Single Whip Reform stimulated the development of the commodity economy to a considerable extent, creating an opportunity for the commercialization of agriculture. It was only because of the harassment from Japanese pirates that the government imposed a maritime ban, which caused a depression in maritime trade.

In the early Qing, the government institutionally restrained commerce out of fear the increasingly prosperous Han people would overthrow their rule. By the time of the Yongzheng era, industry & commerce were neither encouraged nor suppressed while agriculture-oriented policies were adopted. Commercialization grew steadily based on relatively stable agricultural production, though it also helped meet the extravagant demands of the ruling class. The policy was based on the premise that their rule was not threatened. For this reason, the Qing government implemented a ban on maritime trade, which was not removed until the 23rd year of the Kangxi era (1684). Nevertheless, there were still complex regulations and strict bans on major handicrafts, agricultural and sideline products. Silk, iron and shipbuilding industries, that had huge commercialization potential and were important components of the national economy, were restrained for a long time.

In terms of inland trade, a large number of specialized commercial cities emerged, including the silk cities of Suzhou, Hangzhou, and Jiangning, and porcelain cities such as Jingdezhen. At the same time, financial institutions like old-style private banks sprang up. Commodities mainly included raw materials and consumer goods such as cotton, cloth, silk, silk fabrics, porcelain, tobacco, salt and ironware. They were sold in large quantities over long distances.

In general, since the Ming era, agriculture had created enough surplus to support the development of industry and commerce. However, supporting agriculture and relegating commerce, coupled with the maritime ban, hindered the commercialization and industrialization of the economy.

Section 3   Evidence from Japan

I.   *Evolution of Industrial Structure*

Japan established an agricultural society after the introduction of China's agriculture and handicraft technology. Later, with agricultural development and commercialization, Japan turned to industrialization due to pressure from internal affairs and external troubles, bringing an end to agricultural society. This process specifically includes three stages: i) The rise of agriculture: from the 2nd century BC, when agriculture was introduced from China to Japan, to the 7th century; ii) Agricultural peak: from the mid-7th century, when China's economic system was introduced to Japan, to the Sengoku Period in the 16th century; and iii) Commercialization of agriculture: from the implementation of "smallholder autonomy" at the end of the 16th century until the Meiji Period. In this stage, agriculture was both advanced and eroded, with its share tending to decline before industrialization took off.

Industrial structure evolution in Japan's agricultural society has two basic characteristics: i) As in China, agriculture occupied a dominant position. Agricultural prosperity coincided with economic growth; and ii) Agriculture saw its share rise and then decline; handicraft gradually developed in the long term; and commerce gained momentum. The development process of the three sectors is briefly described as follows.

II. Dominance of Agriculture

The Jomon Period spanned from Japan's Paleolithic period thousands of years ago to China's Qin and Han dynasties. At the time, there was no industry in the strict sense, despite the hypothesis of primitive farming culture,[1] which was largely just an extension of plant harvesting.[2]

In the Yayoi Period (300 BC–300 AD). Around the 2nd century BC, Japan was highly influenced by new cultures from

China.[3] Such influence became more noticeable after Emperor Wu established the four commanderies on the Korean peninsula in 108 BC. As a result, Japan gradually moved from primitive harvesting to an irrigated agricultural economy.

In the mid-7th century, China's administration was characterized by central authority; this took effect in Japan. In 646, Japan establish the Ritsuryō system. It also implemented the Handen Shuju system (periodic reallocations of rice fields) and the So-yo-cho system (consisting of taxes on fields, cloth, or local products, and a labor corvee), thus establishing agriculture's central position.

Owing to new technology from China as well as concerted efforts from influential families, Japanese agriculture advanced significantly. Iron tools became popular, and seedling and transplanting methods became commonplace. Oxen and horses were widely used and irrigation facilities were gradually upgraded; there was also an increase in various crop species, forming a rice-centered structure.

From the early Heian Period in the 8th and 9th centuries to the late 16th century, agricultural production was mostly undertaken by communities of geo-organizations on the basis of smallholder autonomy. The adaptation to low agricultural productivity raised agriculture in the Japanese economy to its peak, until the middle Edo Period.

From a production technology perspective, new tools such as rakes and picks emerged; cattle farming also became popular; and construction and irrigation technologies were improved, supporting the construction of large dams and waterwheels.

Agricultural fertilizers such as cattle manure were applied; double cropping wheat and soybeans became quite common, and further, triple cropping of wheat, soybeans and wheat took shape. Tea was cultivated extensively since being introduced in the Nara Period (8th century). Sericulture also kept developing, but began to decline when silk cloth was no longer included in tributes. Hemp as the main clothing material for farmers was produced on a large scale, and cotton was introduced; a variety of local products were developed as commercial crops; cropland was expanded, doubling from the Enchō Era (920) to the Keichō Era (1600). Labor productivity did not change much during this time.

After entering the Edo Period, the smallholder farming principles and the hereditary status system came into effect. Agriculture progressed to some extent, driven by specialization on an institutional level; production tools and crop varieties were refined; agricultural production became labor intensive, which led to agricultural surplus; farmers were prompted to participate in the circulation system, and gradually became central to production. Consequently, the entire economy was commercialized. Simultaneously, division of labor within agriculture in different regions occurred. In particular, the increase in cotton-producing areas further enlarged economic surplus. Moreover, land ownership of farmers gradually expanded with their actual possession of products.

In the late Edo Period, the focus of production shifted to cash crops as a result of agricultural commercialization. Grain production was reduced while population stagnated or even decreased, reducing the status of agriculture.

III. Subordination of Handicraft

Japan's handicraft industry was also imported from China. In the 4th century, Japan was unified under the Yamato Court. At first, handicraftsmen were categorized as slaves, engaged in production for designated consumption. Moreover, since artifacts or weapons were made largely for royal families, there could not be a large number of exchanges. Therefore, farming was still concurrently necessary and superior to handicraft, entrenching this position.

In the Medieval Period, handicrafts were neither completely separated from agriculture, nor liberated from sovereign subordination. Most handicrafts for personal use were produced by farmers themselves. A small number of independent handicraftsmen received protection through hard labor or tribute to temples and lords, and then gradually obtained certain monopoly rights or various privileges in product sales or certain areas. Afterwards, ordinary handicraftsmen followed suit. In the 14th century, the seat system was formed during the Muromachi Period, which drove commercial production. In the Sengoku Period, lords and temples were replaced by daimyos. As the commodity economy kept developing, the seat system gradually disintegrated.

In the mid-Edo Period, rural handicrafts saw sprouts of capitalism, and overwhelmed the urban handicraft industry in both quality and quantity. In this regard, the tribute system played a role in boosting local products. Other indispensable contributors included the continuous development of roads nationwide, and the formation of a national commerce network and market economy. With the development of rural small-scale production, this type of commerce was quickly split into two types: i) early capitalist handicraft workshops formed to compete with a large number of small producers; and ii) wholesale cottage industries formed as commercial capital gradually dominated – through organization – the production process of small producers and operators.

IV. Growth of Commerce

Primitive commerce emerged in Japan with the development of agriculture and handicrafts. It extended as far as China, paying tribute instead of serving trade. There were also "markets" within the country, which were no more than places of exchange. At this time, commerce was still in its infancy. Under the Ritsuryō system, commerce developed owning to the improvement of the Chinese measurement system. By drawing on China's approach, Japan's monetary system adopted coinage as currency.

From the Heian Period in the 8ᵗʰ century to the Edo Period, commerce also developed. Regular markets became more frequent, and even daily markets were seen. Exchange was carried out between producers and users before a professional merchant class (businessmen) formed. Merchants largely farmed crops on their own fields or were engaged in handicrafts, so they were not completely independent. Later, business cities sprang up. They served as the center of regular markets in various regions, and gradually formed a unified commodity circulation network. In the late Medieval Period, specialized commodity markets came into existence. Wholesale merchants started from warehousing and transportation, and gradually became independent goods traders and transporters. In addition, merchants also gathered to seek the protection of lords and temples and obtain sales privileges. In a sense, commerce was not completely detached from handicraft.

Overseas trade in this period mainly targeted the Song, Yuan and Ming dynasties. Currency developed significantly based on the introduction of Chinese copper coins. As the number of privately minted coins and the amount of currency in circulation increased, tributes also became monetized. Loan sharks extended from the storage industry to the pawn industry. At the same time, they accumulated massive monetary capital by operating hotels and sauce shops, and even seized land by executing the power of acting officials.

In the Edo Period, merchants initially could only buy tribute rice from, and sell handicrafts to, lords. However, with the emergence and increase of surplus farm products, commercial farming came into being. Some farmers continuously accumulated wealth and became rich by processing and trading surplus products from surrounding farmers. Landlords rose like parasites, who no longer directly engaged in production and management, but occupied all or part of the surplus labor of farmers through private arable land. In line with the general trend, the shogunate decided to abolish all penalties related to land trading in 1744, making farmland trade completely free. Land contracting by merchants was stimulated, and many hiring laws were introduced. Commercialization at this stage sowed the seeds of capitalism.

Notes

1. Eiichi Fujimori, *Jyoumon Agriculture* (Students' Press, 1970).

2. Hiroshi Tsude, "Agricultural Community and Single-head Power," *Lectures on the History of Japan 1* (University of Tokyo Press, 1970).

3. Kazuo Yamaguchi, *Economic History of Japan* (Chikuma Shobo, 1973).

CHAPTER 5

Evidence from Reality: Industrial Society

In an industrial society, industry plays a major role in economic development relative to other sectors such as agriculture and commerce. Correspondingly, the industrial sector dominates industrial structure. The rise in the share of industry has an inevitable causal influence on economic growth. Industrial structure shows the following trend here: industry advances wave-on-wave while maintaining a dominant position; agriculture develops slowly for a long time; and commerce fluctuates with industry.

This study looks into 19 countries representative of industrial society. More importantly, these economies advance by leaps and bounds, all driven by the rapid development of the industrial sector. This is of vital significance.

Section 1 Evolution of Industrial Structure

As in an agricultural society, the generation, development, evolution and shift of the central sector in an industrial society all result from contradictions among productivity, production relations, and social material and spiritual needs in a certain historical period. They reflect quantitative and qualitative changes contributing to the progress of industrial technology. However, compared with agriculture, industrial has undergone huge changes in social and environmental conditions. Since the First Industrial Revolution, the entire world economy has been integrated by mechanized industrial production.

Firstly, with the improvement of agricultural productivity, most basic material needs can be gradually secured. The expansion of social material and spiritual needs is infinite: these needs are satisfied by the continuous development and conservation of energy and materials, the continuous improvement of product quality and performance, and the continuous reduction of labor costs. Hence, the necessity of the industrial sector is constantly increased.

Secondly, from the perspective of productivity, industrial society presupposes that agricultural productivity has developed to a certain level. But in fact, far before reaching this level, many economies were brought into the world economic system, which was dominated by mechanized industries in the midst of the First Industrial Revolution that began in Britain. Consequently, they had to first serve as agricultural countries in the international system. In order to shake off disadvantages in international trade, agricultural countries must transform into industrial countries by relying on faster industrial development. In the absence of agricultural support, the pursuit of industrial progress would inevitably entail the intermediation and advancement of production relations. This is the case in Japan. In contrast, the United States followed the American-style road to industrialization that begins from agriculture, setting an industrialization model with little institutional interference.

Thirdly, in an industrial society, the quantitative and qualitative changes in industrial technology determine the continuous and spiral development, with fluctuations, in economic and social dimensions. After the central position of industry is established in a country, industrial technology will far exceed agriculture in both speed and intensity of quantitative and qualitative change. Nevertheless, this does not fundamentally solve the contradiction between productivity and social material and spiritual needs, but rather makes the contradiction more complicated. On the one hand, social demand expands beyond existing productivity, however, on the other hand, productivity improvement intensifies the contradiction between productivity and social effective demand.

Productivity in agriculture has made qualitative progress due to the advancement of industrialization, but with very limited depth and breadth compared to industry. The subsequent volatility of agriculture is not significant. On the contrary, industrial productivity has made great strides during the industrial revolutions; it has been largely immune to the influence of natural cycles, and natural and man-made disasters.

Economic ups and downs caused by such external factors do not dominate. Moreover, state intervention in the economic cycle has reduced the impact of structural economic crises. In the long run, economic fluctuations caused by crises are not as significant as they were before WWII.

In this way, changes in production technology become prominent in long-term economic fluctuations. Looking back at world economic history, the prosperity of every industrial society is accompanied by the rapid growth of industry, and characterized by the transformation of its production technology. It is through industrial revolution that many countries jump ahead successfully.

Fourthly, from the perspective of industrial structure, the stagnation of production technology before, the qualitative change during, and the stable development after industrial revolution (as well as stagnation before the next industrial revolution) constitute a trough-shaped trend in industry. Every rise and fall is unavoidable in this process. Regardless of the length and magnitude of the trough, it will not prevent the inevitable emergence of industrial revolution – nor does it mean the industrial sector no longer plays a central role. This has been proved by the industrialization process of various countries like Japan and the United States.

Section 2   Evidence from the United States

I.   *Long-term Industrial Structure Trend*

The United States was relatively late to industrialize compared to much of Europe – partly because it was a British colony until gaining independence. Nevertheless, the long-term trend of the US industrial structure still showed very similar characteristics to Britain. Primary industry as a proportion of the US economy tended to decline in the long run, with ups and downs corresponding to the tertiary industry. Meanwhile, secondary

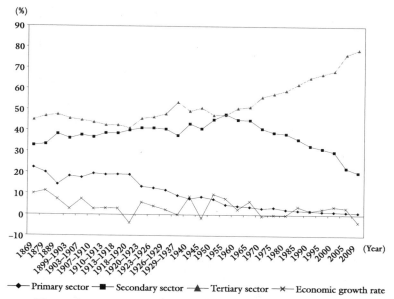

Figure 5.1   Economic Growth and Industrial Structure in the United States

industry has generally gone through two cycles: i) From the late 1860s to the mid-20th century. Industry made up a large share of the economy from the late 19th century to the 1930s off the back of the First Industrial Revolution and advanced the Second Industrial Revolution. The increase of its share in the 1940s was a result of the war economy, rather than an economic long wave; ii) From 1945 to the present, since the US is the birthplace of the Third Industrial Revolution, its secondary industry share once again rose from low to high, peaking between the mid-1940s to early 1970s. Like the UK, the long-term trend of the tertiary industry in the US is not a one-off peak-trough-peak process. Its share has experienced two cycles in terms of value: i) From the late 1860s to the mid-20th century. At first, it grew with the secondary industry to peak in the 1880s, then declined massively, reaching a trough in the 1920s; it then rebounded to peak in the 1930s before decreasing in the war economy; ii) From the 1940s to present. It fell in the mid-1950s, and then rose all the way to over 50% of GDP. The long-term trend of US industrial structure has proved Clark's Law wrong, as shown in Figure 5.1.[1]

II. First Cycle

The North American continent was "discovered" by Christopher Columbus in the late 15th century. Due to contradictions escalated by British repression and exploitation along with economic development, the American War of Independence broke out in 1775, and the United States was formally established in 1783.

Later on, the technological revolution in agriculture began around 1820. Simultaneously, land nationalization and farmer autonomy was realized by confiscating residual land from feudalists, plundering and annexing American Indian land westward, and purchasing and annexing British, Spanish, and French colonies in North America and large tracts of land in Mexico. As Lincoln signed the *Homestead Act* in 1862, legislation finally allowed the free distribution of state-owned land in the west, and facilitated the completion of American-style roads characterized by an upturn in agriculture.

In terms of industry, machinery such as hydraulic spinning machines and power looms were brought to the US after 1790, leading to the industrial revolution. In 1860, industrial output value surpassed that of agriculture in the north; in the south, progress was slower, with a breakthrough achieved only after the Civil War (1861–1865). In this way, the nationwide industrial revolution was basically over by the 1880s.

Over time, the US became established as an industrial center. By industrial production, it ranked fifth in the world in 1840 and fourth in 1860. At this time, the industrial output value of the United States was $1.9 billion, compared to $2.8 billion for Britain. By 1894, the United States had the world's largest industrial output – nearly $9.5 billion, more than twice that of Britain. At the beginning of the 20th century, with the formation and development of monopolies, the industrial sector leveraged trusts to strengthen its economic domination. In 1913, the United States contributed 38% of global industrial output, equivalent to the sum of Britain, France, Germany and Japan combined. Such growth reached a climax in the 1920s. Following the Great Depression in the 1930s, the United States, a war profiteer from

WWII, strengthened technological research & development and initiated the Third Technological Revolution.

III. Second Cycle

From WWII to the late 1950s, the US carried out arms expansion and war preparations by stepping up technological development and utilization. The excess profits brought about by technological advancement encouraged producers to continue pursuing new industrial technologies. Consequently, the industrial sector drove the entire economy into the second peak. This round of technological revolution transformed traditional industries such as coal, metallurgy, textiles, automobiles, machine manufacturing and food processing, giving rise to emerging industries such as nuclear energy, marine, and microelectronics industries. It also triggered a consumer revolution that made automobiles and household appliances commonplace.

In the 1950s, the United States began to vigorously prop up industrial progress in capitalist countries, especially Japan and Germany, for the purpose of maintaining the Cold War system. To a certain extent, the practice did promote industrial progress, but the US was eventually burdened from supporting entire economies and markets. With the industrial technology transfer to emerging industrial countries, US imports shifted to cheaper industrial products manufactured by these technologies, causing American industry to gradually shrank. This prompted the US, under huge global pressure, to launch the New Economic Policy in 1971. Since the collapse of the Bretton Woods system, which tied currencies to a gold standard and pegged them to the US dollar, the United States has fallen into chronic depression.

Through long-term adjustments, the US restored economic prosperity in the mid-1980s with the help of hi-tech industry. Such a relatively long period of prosperity was fundamentally attributed to the faster development of industry through industrial revolution that altered the original production system. The long-term downward trend in industry stopped, instead maintaining a reasonable share, and curbing the increase in service sector share. However, it is not difficult to see that with the small rise in services, the real growth rate of the entire economy also begun to decline slightly.

To sum up, the evolution of industrial structure in the United States has two characteristics: i) In the period of rapid economic growth, the share of industry in the national economy was rising. At this time, agriculture tended to decline slowly because it was replaced by the more efficient industrial sector. Services, which supports the operation of industry, developed alongside it. Its share also went up and down with that of industry; ii) In the long run, under the impetus of successive industrial revolutions, the industrial sector grew in a wave pattern, as did the service sector that is subordinate to industry.

Section 3   Evidence from Canada

With a vast territory, Canada is rich in hydraulic, forestry, and mineral resources. As early as WWI, Canada stimulated development of the non-ferrous metal sector by providing the Allied Powers with munitions, but it plunged into crisis with the end of the war. Canada was also not immune to the global depression that broke out in 1929. After joining WWII, Canada prospered again from military demand, and moved away from Britain and towards the US in foreign economic relations, paving an important foundation for post-war development.

Canada developed rapidly after the war. In 1950, its GDP totaled $17.48 billion and $1,272 per capita – equivalent to

Table 5.1   Economic Growth and Industrial Structure in Canada

Unit: billion CA$, %

Year	GDP	Proportion of agricultural sector	Proportion of industrial sector	Proportion of service sector	GDP growth rate
1973	344.56	3.6	35.8	60.6	–
1975	365.63	3.3	32.3	64.4	2.1
1978	419.56	3.1	31.6	65.3	4.3
1980	440.98	2.9	30.9	66.2	1.3
1983	456.54	3.1	29.6	67.3	3.2
1985	508.45	2.7	30.5	66.8	4.7
1988	573.39	2.5	29.9	67.6	4.9
1990	585.77	2.8	28.8	68.4	–0.3
1993	591.43	7.0	26.5	66.5	2.3
1996	–	7.1	26.7	66.1	1.6

Note: Data for years earlier than 1990 are converted by the 1987 prices and data for years after 1990 converted by 1986 prices.
Source: International Bureau of the Bank of Japan, *International Comparative Statistics*.

68% of the US level. In 1982, the numbers climbed to $299.68 billion and $12,167 respectively, almost level with the US per capita, and making Canada one of the seven major capitalist nations globally.

However, Canada experienced a long period of stagflation after the oil crisis. It fell into severe economic recession in the early 1980s and did not recover until 1983. By September 1990, Canada had sustained economic growth for about nine years, creating the longest period of economic expansion after the war. In this process, industry always played a major role in driving growth and maintained a relatively high proportion of the economy. After 1992, the Canadian economy began to grow again, but the share of the industrial sector exhibited a downward trend, as shown in Table 5.1.

Section 4   Evidence from Mexico

Mexico is located at the southern tip of the North American continent. It is endowed with abundant mineral resources such as oil, diverse agricultural, forest and animal husbandry resources as well as excellent fishery resources with great development potential.

Mexico secured an average annual economic growth rate of 6–7% from the 1950s–80s. This is attributed to the growth of industry and the modernization of agriculture. The next long period of economic growth arrived after the mid-1980s, which was also driven by industry growth.

From the early 1950s to the early 80s, agriculture as a share of GDP dropped from 20 to 9.3%, while the share of industry increased considerably, with manufacturing alone climbing from 17.8 to 24.1%. Thus, Mexico gradually evolved from a basic agricultural and mining producer, and exporter, to an emerging industrial nation with a diverse and relatively complete economic structure.

In the early 1980s, Mexico's debt problems were exposed. In August 1982, the country could not repay the interest on its foreign debts, and the economy thereafter plunged into

Table 5.2   Economic Growth and Industrial Structure in Mexico

Unit: billion Mexican Peso, %

Year	GDP	Proportion of agricultural sector	Proportion of industrial sector	Proportion of service sector	GDP growth rate
1973	115.29	10.4	35.5	54.3	–
1975	129.25	9.7	35.5	54.8	5.7
1978	150.52	9.6	36.3	54.1	8.2
1980	178.22	8.5	37.4	54.1	8.4
1983	184.55	8.7	35.1	56.2	–4.2
1985	196.59	8.7	36.2	55.1	2.7
1988	195.26	8.3	36.4	55.3	1.0
1990	210.54	9.0	37.6	54.4	4.2
1993	225.63	7.6	37.3	55.1	0.4

Note: GDP growth rate is the ratio of GDP of the current year to that of the previous year.
Source: International Bureau of the Bank of Japan, *International Comparative Statistics.*

long-term crisis and depression. A series of policy adjustments such as fiscal tightening, inflation control, stimulating private investment, and improving economic efficiency, were combined with various economic and social development plans to restore economic stabilization. In the mid- to late 1980s, with the success of debt negotiations, Mexico's credit rating began to recover, and demonstrated vitality again with foreign capital inflows. The economic growth was also driven by industry, manifesting in changes in industry, as show in Table 5.2.

Section 5   Evidence from Britain

Britain was the birthplace of the First Industrial Revolution and the first nation to industrialize. In the long run, Britain's industrial structure did not change in the way Clark described – i.e., the primary, secondary and tertiary industries take turns to occupy a dominant share. More specifically, the share of primary industry exhibited a long-term reduction. There were only short-term fluctuations in the share of secondary industry at the beginning of industrialization, which reflects the fact that it had not yet secured a dominant position.

This share did not go up and down only once, but experienced three cycles under the impetus of industrial revolutions: i) From the mid-18th to the mid-19th century, including the First Industrial Revolution. The highest share appeared at the prosperity stage between the 1820s and 1830s; ii) From the mid-19th to the mid-20th century, including the Second Industrial

Revolution. The peak share was observed at the beginning of the 20th century; and iii) From the mid-20th century to the present, including the Third Industrial Revolution. This peaked during the 1950s–70s. The tertiary industry share did not rise and fall only once, but went through two cycles: i) The share fluctuated with that of the primary industry in the short run, and peaked in the mid-20th century. Fluctuations were not significant during this period because the tertiary industry could still not meet the needs of Britain as the world factory, and advanced with the secondary industry; ii) After the mid-20th century, the driving force of tertiary industry was weakened as Britain gradually lost its global industrial dominance, halting the increase of its share. Afterwards, its share fluctuated against the secondary industry, as shown in Figure 5.2.[2]

As we can see, neither the secondary and tertiary industries as a proportion of the British economy changed in the way described by Clark. There are three main reasons for this: i) Clark used data from the early 19th century to around the 1930/40s, covering the end of the First Industrial Revolution and all of the Second Industrial Revolution. Due to historical limitations, he could see the sudden changes to industrial structure caused by the Third Industrial Revolution; ii) In Clark's early research period, the decline of industry between the first and second industrial revolutions was not clear. Later, the benefits of industrial revolution gradually arose in Europe and the United States. As the world's hegemon, British industry sustained growth by taking advantage of global industrial development. If not for the First Industrial Revolution, Clark would have classified this period as a

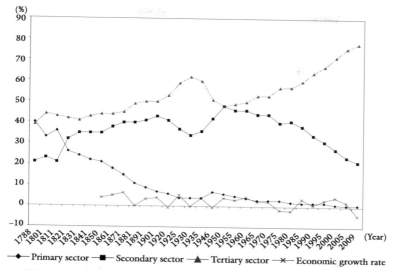

Figure 5.2   Economic Growth and Industrial Structure in Britain

single long cycle; and iii) Clark mostly studied industrial structure in the long run, thus to some extent ignoring fluctuations in each stage. In contrast, this study notices the rebound of secondary industry share since the mid-20th century.

Section 6   Evidence from the Federal Republic of Germany

Germany's industrial structure shows similar long-term trends to Britain and the United States: its primary industry share declined in the long run; the share of secondary industry went through

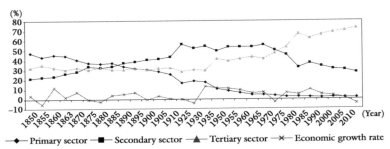

Figure 5.3   Economic Growth and Industrial Structure in Germany

two cycles, with the mid-20th century as the dividing line, as did the tertiary industry share. The difference is that during the first cycle, the share of the tertiary industry changed very little; in Germany, the tertiary industry did not dominate the industrial structure in the mid-19th century, as in Britain and the US – it took up a higher share than secondary industry, but less than primary industry. Therefore, tertiary industry could not satisfy economic growth demands in the first long industrialization cycle. It developed along with secondary industry in the long term. It was not until 1910 that the tertiary industry share dropped sharply as the secondary industry advanced rapidly. In the 1930s, tertiary industry share began to rise due to decline of the secondary industry, reaching a peak in the 1950s. This is shown in Figure 5.3.[3]

From a historical point of view, Germany is a relatively young capitalist country. When Britain was finishing its first industrialization stage in the 1830s, Germany had just begun its industrial revolution. By the beginning of the 20th century,

Germany had achieved industrialization and rose to becomes one of Europe's most powerful nations. After losing the two world wars, in 1918 and 1945 respectively, the country was split in two at the end of WWII. This study mainly investigates West Germany (the Federal Republic of Germany). From the post-war period to the 1970s, West Germany saw extremely rapid economic development, with a growth rate second only to Japan, becoming the third largest power in the capitalist world. Following the outbreak of the oil crisis in early 1970s, economic growth slowed and the industrial share started to drop, though Germany quickly recovered.

The steel, machinery and chemistry sectors were already quite developed before WWII. The industrial sector as a whole advanced more rapidly after the war, with an average annual growth rate of 7% from 1950 to 1973. However, it stagnated after 1974 and began to rebound after the mid-1980s. The average annual growth rate was 0.6% during 1973–1984 and 2.7% during 1984–1991. The reunification of Germany in 1990 initially created a lot of demand for western industry, but put a heavy burden on the whole nation. On the one hand, the domestic demand market gradually shrank, dwarfed by the quick recovery of the industrial sector of the eastern region. On the other hand, the international environment for Germany deteriorated. While the US industrial sector gained increasing competitiveness owning to rapid development in the 1990s, other countries such as Japan were still in crisis. In addition, the high interest rate policy and tax increases adopted by the German government dampened investment and personal consumption, which was responsible for the economic stagnation and recession. Although the economy of former East Germany began to rise out of the slump in 1992, the German economy was still sluggish on the whole, with economic growth contracting after a short-term rise in 1991. In the mid-1990s, the German economy began to recover. With the advent of the single European currency (the Euro) in 1998, the Deutsche Mark, as the main base currency of the Euro, assumes greater responsibility, putting even heavier pressure on the German economy.

Section 7 Evidence from Italy

Some of the first seeds of capitalism in Europe sprouted in Italy during the Renaissance period in the 14th and 15th centuries. However, its industrialization proceeded very slowly. According to statistics, the transformation of its industrial structure is also not a single cycle as described by Clark. In particular, the share of the primary industry declined in the long run. The sharp increase around 1945 should be regarded as a special phenomenon because the secondary and tertiary industries were destroyed by the war. The secondary industry experienced at least two cycles, with 1945 as the dividing line. It is similar for the tertiary industry. Although we do not know whether change prior to 1990 should be counted as a cycle or not due to the absence of statistical data, there has already been sufficient proof that Clark's Law is not accurate, as shown in Figure 5.4.[4]

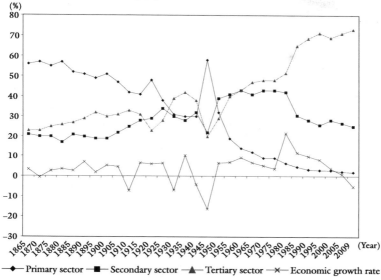

Figure 5.4　Economic Growth and Industrial Structure in Italy

Located in southern Europe, Italy represents an ancient civilization. Despite the earliest signs of capitalism, its development was relatively slow. At the end of WWII, Italy still lagged economically far behind other major capitalist countries in Europe. Afterwards, driven by the fast-growing industrial sector, the national economy developed so rapidly that Italy had transformed from a basic agricultural and industrial nation to a highly industrialized one, becoming the world's sixth largest economy. As the share of services increased steeply after the 1990s, there was a post-industrial tendency in Italy which caused the slowdown of economic growth. Italy's actual economic growth rate dropped from 2.2% in 1990 to 0.7% in 1996, according to the *International Comparative Statistics* compiled by the International Bureau of the Bank of Japan.

After WWII, Italy was among the poorest in Europe with an extremely fragile economic foundation. For this reason, the Italian government strengthened economic regulation and intervention, established an open economic system, and actively explored the international market. With strong American support to the European economy, combined with appropriate domestic policy stimulus, Italy's economy kept growing. From 1950 to 1963, its average annual GDP growth rate registered 5.9%, second only to Germany in Europe – this is considered an economic miracle. In 1964, an economic crisis interrupted the rapid growth. From 1965 to 1973, average annual GDP growth fell to 5.2%, but still ranked amongst the top in Europe. In the 1970s, the oil crisis and the global economic crisis significantly impaired its speed of development. From 1973 to 1980, the rate was only 2.8%. The slowdown continued as a serious economic crisis broke out in early 1980s, lasting till 1985.

In the process mentioned above, industry played a decisive role. Economic prosperity was accompanied by fast development of industry, while economic slumps were caused by industrial slowdown. Italy's industrial sector was restored to its pre-war level in 1948, and has since entered a period of rapid expansion. From 1951 to 1960, the average annual growth rate of industrial production reached 8.8%. It dropped to 7.2% during 1961–1970, 3.5% during 1971–1980, and 1.9% during 1980–1990. It is evident there is a very close relationship between decline in industrial share and slowdown of overall economic growth after 1975. This suggests that the industrial sector remains the decisive force of the entire economy; the so-called post-industrial society does not exist in reality.

Section 8   Evidence from France

France has the largest territory among Western European nations. Fertile soil in most areas, a mild climate, and abundant rainfall provide excellent natural conditions for agriculture and animal husbandry. France boasts the largest reserves of iron ore, bauxite and uranium ore in Europe, but almost entirely depends on imports for oil.

France is an old capitalist country. The agricultural sector was already highly developed before WWII. The industrial sector developed rapidly after the war's end with support from the US and European economies. In the midst of post-war capitalist development, France became the fourth largest industrial nation after the United States, Japan, and Germany.

In terms of industrial structure, industry took up a high share before the mid-1970s, but the share dropped steeply after the mid-1970s, leading to a sharp fall in the annual GDP growth rate. This illustrates the importance of industry. On the contrary, the service sector has seen rapid growth since the mid-1970s, with its share reaching about 75% in 1994, as shown in Figure 5.5.[5]

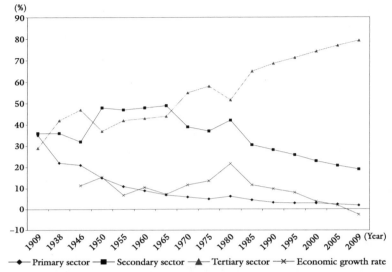

Figure 5.5 Economic Growth and Industrial Structure in France

Section 9 Evidence from Sweden

Situated in northern Europe, Sweden has abundant water resources such as dense lakes, turbulent rivers and many waterfalls, as well as rich iron ore, forests, and uranium resources. In the mid-19th century, Sweden was still a poor agricultural country. Later, it grew gradually into an industrially developed country, owing to the long-term pursuit of the peace principle and stable economic policy. In particular, the mixed economic system adopted since WWII has facilitated the relatively long-term and stable development of Sweden's economy.

The industrial sector is relatively developed and occupies a very important position in the national economy. After WWII, steel, wood processing, shipbuilding and textiles developed rapidly as Sweden's main export industries. However, industrial production took a long-term downward trend following the outbreak of the two oil crises in the early 1970s. Industry did not begin to recover until 1983 as traditional industries gradually gave way to machinery manufacturing, precise electronic instruments, and automobiles. In order to stimulate the industrial sector, the Swedish government set up a huge enterprise renewal fund to

Table 5.3   Industrial Structure and Economic Growth in Sweden

Unit: billion kronor, %

Year	GDP	Proportion of agricultural sector	Proportion of industrial sector	Proportion of service sector	GDP growth rate
1973	791.8	3.8	31.9	64.3	–
1975	835.4	3.4	31.2	65.4	2.4
1978	842.5	3.3	29.5	67.2	1.6
1980	889.1	3.2	29.7	67.1	1.7
1983	914.9	3.5	29.5	67.0	2.0
1985	970.8	3.3	30.8	65.9	1.9
1988	1046.3	2.9	30.7	66.4	2.2
1990	1086.5	3.2	30.1	66.7	1.4
1993	1030.7	–	–	–	–2.6

Note: GDP growth rate is the ratio of GDP of the current year to that of the previous year.
Source: International Bureau of the Bank of Japan, *International Comparative Statistics*.

support technological innovation, equipment renewal, research personnel training, and high-level technological openings. Meanwhile, it strengthened capital concentration and urged enterprise reorganization and mergers. These policies created a solid cornerstone of economic stability by effectively curbing the decline in industrial share.

Judging from the long-term trend of industrial structure as shown in Table 5.3, industry has not seen rapid growth since the 1970s, and its share has remained around 30% for a long time; thus, the overall economy exhibits low-speed growth in the long term.

Section 10   Evidence from Belgium

Located in western Europe, Belgium embraces coal as its main economic resource. Historically, Belgium has always relied on industry such as coal mining, steelmaking and textiles. As these traditional industries gradually gave way to emerging industries after WWII, Belgium saw rapid economic growth.

The Belgian economy recovered quickly after the war. Especially since the 1960s, the Belgian government adopted policies to open the economy to global markets and vigorously absorb foreign investment, bringing financial impetus to the country and giving rise to new industries and technologies. Petroleum, chemicals, electronics and nuclear energy industries have risen rapidly, replacing traditional industries to occupy a dominant position in the national economy.

The average annual GDP growth rate was 2.4% in the 1950s and climbed to 4.8% in the 1960s. Economic growth slowed to 3.6% in the 1970s due to the oil crisis and plummeted to 0.3% during 1980–1982. The economy began to rebound slowly after 1983, with an average growth rate of 1.3% from 1982 to 1987, and then tended to decrease again in the 1990s. There is a very close relationship between economic growth and industrial structure, and especially industrial sector growth. Industrial output value in 1987 increased by 1.93 times compared with 1950, marking an average annual growth rate of 3%. From 1960

Table 5.4 Industrial Structure and Economic Growth in Belgium

Unit: billion Belgian Franc, %

Year	GDP	Proportion of agricultural sector	Proportion of industrial sector	Proportion of service sector	GDP growth rate
1973	4064.0	–	–	–	–
1975	4167.3	1.9	29.6	68.5	–1.5
1978	4551.6	1.9	30.5	67.6	2.8
1980	4845.7	1.g	30.3	67.9	4.2
1983	4893.1	2.0	30.0	68.0	0.6
1985	5041.4	2.1	29.7	68.2	0.8
1988	5468.0	2.0	30.0	68.0	4.9
1990	5844.2	1.8	30.9	67.3	3.3
1993	5983.4	–	–	–	–1.7

Note: GDP growth rate is the ratio of GDP of the current year to that of the previous year.
Source: International Bureau of the Bank of Japan, *International Comparative Statistics.*

to 1970, the industrial sector grew at an average annual rate of 5%. However, the rate was only 0.7% from 1973 to 1981 as the industrial sector expanded by 4.7% in total, considering the stagnation of industrial production in 1974 and 1975 due to the economic crisis. With the slow recovery of industry from 1982 onwards, the average annual growth rate reached 3.6% from 1982 to 1987, but dropped to 1.4% from 1988 to 1991. As shown in Table 5.4, the relationship between the share of the industrial sector and economic growth is even more obvious.

Section 11   Evidence from Greece

Greece is located in the southern Balkan Peninsula and is rich in mineral resources such as lignite and aluminum. It is one of the ancient civilizations of the world and the cradle of European culture. Until the 1950s, Greece was still an agricultural society. However, driven by the rapid development of industry, its economic structure underwent major change. Before this, Greece mainly produced tobacco, cotton, and sugar beets. At the time, agriculture contributed to more than 40% of the national economy, while industry accounted for less than 25%. This changed in the 1960s and 1970s. Traditional industries such as food, tobacco, textiles and tanning gradually gave way to heavy chemical industries such as metallurgy, chemicals, oil refining and shipbuilding. Among them, manufacturing grew at an average annual rate of 7.9% from 1950 to 1960 and 9.8% from 1960 to 1973. Due to the economic crisis in 1973 and 1974,

Table 5.5 Industrial Structure and Economic Growth in Greece

Unit: billion Greek Zamak, %

Year	GDP	Proportion of agricultural sector	Proportion of industrial sector	Proportion of service sector	GDP growth rate
1973	4582.4	19.2	33.4	47.4	–
1975	4670.5	20.9	30.8	48.3	2.9
1978	5499.4	17.9	31.9	50.2	6.6
1980	5797.1	18.0	31.3	50.7	1.5
1983	5850.3	16.3	29.9	53.8	0.6
1985	6194.9	16.8	29.6	53.6	3.1
1988	6549.4	16.5	29.8	53.3	4.4
1990	5725.9	13.7	29.5	56.8	–0.8
1993	6965.5	–	–	–	–0.5

Note: GDP growth rate is the ratio of GDP of the current year to that of the previous year.
Source: International Bureau of the Bank of Japan, *International Comparative Statistics*.

industrial progress slowed, with the average rate shrinking to 2.2% in this period, and even 1.0% from 1987 to 1991. Table 5.5 also indicates that since 1975, the share of industry has tended to decline slowly, and the rate of economic growth overall has been low.

Section 12 Evidence from Japan

I. Long-term Evolution

As a latecomer, Japan spent 100 years traversing the 200-year course of older capitalist countries such as Britain, and grew from a semi-colonial nation into the world's second largest economy. In this process of leapfrog development, the industrial sector mainly experienced two upsurges and two cycles. The first cycle was from 1868 to 1945, with an upsurge from 1905 to 1920. In this cycle, the fast development of industry was driven by institutional advancement and unchecked foreign aggression and plunder. The second cycle was from 1945 to the 1990s, with an upsurge from 1955 to 1970. In this cycle, rapid in-dustrial growth rested on institutional progress and a favorable international environment. More specifically, since Japan began industrialization through Meiji Restoration, the primary industry share has declined in the long term. The increase around 1945 resulted from the depression of the secondary and tertiary industries caused by WWII.

The secondary and tertiary industry shares also exhibited two cycles each, with 1945 as the dividing line. The share of secondary industry increased continuously in the first cycle because Japan enlarged industrial production forcibly in order to meet the demands of war; such growth should not be deemed as natural economic development. In addition, the secondary industry was already in a state of decay when the war ended, though direct evidence of this may unavailable due to lack of data. Nevertheless, the data for 1950 and 1955 – during the recovery

124

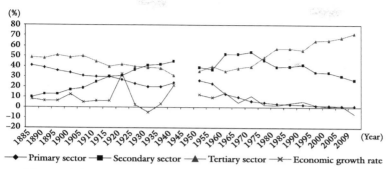

Figure 5.6   Economic Growth and Industrial Structure in Japan

period – suggests the secondary industry share in 1945 should be much lower. Besides, as aforementioned, major industrial nations experienced a new long cycle after 1945. Therefore, there were two long cycles in the secondary and tertiary industries of Japan, as shown in Figure 5.6.[6] This proves the single-cycle view of Clark's Law wrong.

II.   Trend by Sectors

Japan's rapid development was mainly driven by two upsurges of secondary industry. The first occurred during 1905–1920, when GDP increased fourfold. The contribution of the secondary industry ascended from 21.1% in 1905 to 31.6% in 1930, while the tertiary industry share fell from 46% to 40.17% in 1920. The second upsurge spanned from 1955 to 1970. During this period, gross national product (GNP) expanded at an annual average rate of 9.7%, and manufacturing grew at an even higher rate of 13–24%. The contribution of secondary industry climbed from 23.5% in 1955 to 40% in 1970.[7] This process also verified the positive correlation between the secondary sector and economic growth, as revealed in the United States, Britain and other countries.

Industrial structure in Japan has two long run characteristics caused by industrialization: i) Industry plays a central role. Rapid economic growth was also accompanied by the upsurge of industry, driven by technological progress and manifested in its rising share. And vice versa, when industry declined, economic growth slowed down or even slipped into depression. This implies industry is the main driving force of economic growth; ii) The share of industry and services fluctuated alternately with wave-like undulation, while the share of agriculture exhibited a downward long-term trend.

Analysis may be undermined if data analysis is limited to the start and end years, so the specific course of development is examined below by sectors.

1. The share of the agricultural sector declined in the long term.

Except for the first ten years (before the 1890s), the share of agriculture has been on a downward trend throughout. The initial expansion of agriculture arose from the need of capital accumulation for industry. After the Meiji Restoration however, agriculture became the largest source of national finance (and at the same time, determined the innate deficiency of capital accumulation). In 1872, land tax accounted for 90.9% and 39.74% of tax revenues and fiscal revenues respectively. The former fell to 75.7% before 1879, but the latter rose to 67.76%.

In this way, agriculture was forcibly incorporated into the commodity economy. A large number of farmers went bankrupt as massive land sales were facilitated, providing a relatively sufficient source of labor. Agriculture then advanced in the form of preparing capital and labor for industry. But later, its support for industry was replaced by the plunder of China and Korea's agricultural sectors, while progress was made in mechanization and chemicalization.

After WWII, focus was shifted towards industrial development as a result of agricultural reform initiated by the General Commander of the Occupation Army (GHQ) in 1946. From 1950 to 1955, a preparation stage for high-speed growth, food shortages remained unresolved, and food security was threatened by the Korean War. Low food self-sufficiency meant a large number of imports, which squeezed funds for importing technology and equipment urgently needed for industrial development. In addition, there was still a large surplus population in rural areas. To this end, an agricultural policy centered on rice and wheat yields increased self-sufficiency. In terms of finance, support was given to group-run water supply and drainage, ranch preparation, and land improvement for corporate farming. There were also financial support policies for specific areas. In terms of funding, an agricultural, forestry, and fishery financial corporation was set up in 1953, putting a long-term, low-profit financing system for land improvement in place. Consequently, agricultural productivity improved considerably, enabling the highest rice yields in Japan's history. The application of chemical fertilizers and the penetration of agricultural machinery increased rapidly; and at the same time, the labor force tended to move away from agriculture.

From 1955 to 1965, an early stage of high-speed growth, agricultural productivity improved markedly, substantially driving up yields of rice, fruit, and animal products; agricultural labor began to flow out. Noticing the increasing pressure of surplus agricultural exports from the US, the Japanese government chose to move away from traditional small-scale self-cultivation farming. It promulgated the *Basic Law on Agriculture* in 1961, adjusting prices to balance supply and demand; and to narrow the labor productivity gap between agriculture and other industries. Price-based fiscal subsidies as well as legal and financial adjustments were arranged to protect and support agriculture, with a view to "independent management" for income equilibrium. In terms of financial subsidies, the "production cost and income compensation method" was used to determine rice prices.

At this stage, reliance on agriculture grew. In terms of productivity, the Agricultural Land Law was amended to lift the restrictions on the maximum area of agricultural land sales and to establish legal person and credit systems for agriculture. In addition, the Agricultural Structure Improvement Project was launched. Given basic crops (rice or other), a total of 2,945 large-scale farms of more than 30 acres were created in one fell swoop, and large-scale equipment such as tractors, weeding machines, combine harvesters, and rice hulling systems was imported, enabling an amazing leap forward. These policies, coupled with the increase in agricultural product imports, agricultural investment and consumption levels, and urbanization, bought down the share of the agricultural population. Simultaneously, the number of specialized farmers dropped sharply, while the number of part-time farmers increased steeply. Farmers whose income was mainly from non-agricultural business outnumbered conventional farmers.

After 1965, agriculture fell into recession. First, amid long-term prosperity, the international balance of payments surplus continued to expand along with a surge in industrial exports. This added pressure from the international community, especially the United States.

For the benefit of industry, Japan opened up part of its agricultural market. The agricultural self-sufficiency rate fell headlong, and agricultural product imports skyrocketed. Second, labor productivity improved markedly because comprehensive mechanization had been truly realized. Third, labor continued to flow out of agriculture as the number of part-time farmers grew; this gave rise to industrial land use tensions and high land prices. Finally, agricultural land shrank as a whole as the rate of desolation exceeded the rate of reclamation, while residential and industrial land use expanded continuously. In 1969, the New National Comprehensive Development Plan aimed to build a central and local intelligence and transportation network to encourage private capital to buy and occupy land, resulting in surging land prices. This made it more difficult to expand the scale of agricultural production because farmers were more inclined to be "landed workers" (part-time farmers). More importantly, the surging land prices suggested that heavy chemical industries had reached a critical point of industrialization. After the oil crisis, the Japanese economy fell into depression on all fronts.

2. The share of the industrial sector went through two cycles of rise and fall, with the peak periods spanning from 1905–1920 and 1955–1970 respectively.

During the Meiji Restoration, Japan began industrialization under the three slogans of "Encourage Industry," "Enrich the Nation and Strengthen the Army," and "Civilization and Enlightenment." First, while forcing the primitive accumulation of agriculture, Japan fully transplanted the capitalist economic and factory systems. A large number of model factories were established. Not only was the Industrial Exhibition held, but industrial laboratories were also created, sending people abroad to learn advanced technology and management experience. At the same time, foreign technology and equipment were introduced and then leased to private enterprise. From 1880 onwards, model factories in all sectors, except the war industry, were transferred almost free of charge to private capital close to the government. This catalyzed the transformation of private commercial capital into industrial capital, established a modern factory system, and paved the way for tycoon formation. Second, through a series of aggressive wars against foreign countries, Japan increased capital accumulation, dumped industrial products at low prices, and plundered agricultural products.

It was based on the aforementioned internal institutional advancement and external plunder that Japan constructed the basic framework of an industrial society, joined the industrial revolution in the late 1880s, and began to take off. At the time, the Second Industrial Revolution was in full swing. By absorbing the fruits of the two industrial revolutions, Japan avoided wasting industrial capital in the steam engine age and directly skipped ahead to the electrical age.

As industrial revolution basically ended after the Russo-Japanese War in the early 20th century, Japan generally realized the localization of production materials. In 1909, cotton exports surpassed imports for the first time in Japan. Benefiting from government support, the concentration of production and capital accelerated notably with the development of heavy chemical industries and the advancement of economic crisis. This opened a prelude to the transition from free competition to monopoly. The outbreak of WWI sparked an all-round investment and production boom in Japan, in which private equipment investment reached its climax in 1920. Japan transformed from a debtor country of 1.09 billion yen to a creditor country of 2.71 billion yen. This exerted an indirect impact on the economy by creating the first peak for industrial share.

In 1920–1921, economic crisis broke out, but in 1924 the economy began to develop slowly. As countries such as France, Germany, the United States, and Britain were also sluggish, the Japanese government did not hesitate to implement the gold standard from January 11, 1930. Three days after the announcement, the US stock market plummeted, triggering a worldwide economic crisis. The economic depression in Japan was exacerbated by the gold standard system. During the Great Depression of the 1930s, exports plunged by 76.5% and imports by 71.7%. The operating rate of all major industrial sectors was below 50%, and the agricultural famine pushed the crisis to its climax. In order to absolve the crisis, the Japanese government tightened control over tycoons and urged the establishment of cartels in 50 industries. Simultaneously, it intensified labor coercion and fired a large number of workers. Against the backdrop of increasingly acute economic contradictions at home and abroad, the Japanese government practiced fascism internally and started a war of aggression against China, leading the entire economy astray.

After the end of WWII, the Japanese economy entered a second cycle. At first, inflation was suppressed but not curbed, due to the serious shortage of raw materials and energy resources. In light of this, with the industrial sector as the focal and breakthrough point, Japan launched the priority production policy in 1947 to vigorously support the coal, electricity, fertilizer, steel, shipping, and textile sectors.

Under such conditions, coupled with the support of US aid, industrial and mining production recovered significantly in Japan, but inflation increased subsequently. In April 1949, GHQ began to forcibly implement the contractionary Dodge Line and Shaup tax system. Soon, prices generally stabilized, but other consequences included extremely scarce financial resources, poor business operations, reduced effective demand, increased stagnant goods, and production stagnancy. In the second half of 1949, the Japanese economy sank into a Dodge crisis. The slump looked worse as the United States was also in crisis at the time. The Korean War, which broke out in June 195,0 allowed Japan to escape the crisis through good fortune. Since then, it has expanded reproduction spurred by "special needs," and was brought back to the international market by the United States.

In 1950, Japan began to rationalize investments in industries such as steel, coal, shipping, electricity, synthetic fibers and fertilizers. Special taxation measures and investment and financing policies were used to support the industrial sector. Simultaneously, government investment in public facilities were concentrated in industrial infrastructure such as roads, harbors, water supply, and communications. On the whole, this set the conditions for Japan's rapid growth later.

From the late 1950s to the early 1970s, with special US support, Japan developed rapidly by introducing a lot of cheap but advanced industrial technology, and practicing industrial rationalization and scaleup policies; the industrial sector witnessed rapid growth. From here, the industrial revolution can be divided into three stages: i) From 1956 to 1961, through the introduction of technology, durable consumer goods emerged such as home appliances, automobiles and synthetic fibers; the electric power industry began to use coal power as the main source and hydropower as a supplement; ii) From 1962 to 1966, large-scale production equipment was developed, new production technologies were widely adopted, and the development and application of new materials were strengthened; and iii) From 1967 to 1974, large-scale production equipment was further developed and applied; production technology integrating electronic computers was adopted; and the computer industry was vigorously developed. During this period, the Japanese economy grew at an average annual rate of 9.7%, manufacturing specifically registered a rate of 13–24%, and the industrial sector increased in share.

3. The share of the service sector fluctuated with other sectors, but the Japanese economy collapsed as a result of excessive expansion of the virtual economy after the 1980s, which still remains bleak in long run.

In the early Meiji era, with key support from the "Encourage Industry" policy, commerce became more active while banking, transportation and communication industries developed tremendously. The service sector occupied a major position in capital and technical aspects until WWI, forming a basic framework from the provision of capital to services for the entire production process. That being so, service contributions to GNP were initially second only to agriculture. Its share declined in the midst of vigorous industrial development from 1905 to 1920, then rebounded due to industrial recession, and gradually shrank due to intensive military development. Such fluctuations in services are dwarfed by the sharp drop in the share of agriculture as a result of colonial plunder.

After WWII, the service sector was included in the circular track of the industrial sector. Relying on government support (excess loan policies), the financial sector provided companies with enormous funds that far exceeded their capital capacity. Commerce, especially foreign trade, grew beyond industrial and mining production, and constituted an important part of the "development through processing trade" policy. The share of services dropped from 1955 to 1970 and rose slightly after 1975. Similarly, the change was dwarfed by the slow development of agriculture. However, in the 1980s, the economic transition from "servitization" to "virtualization" began to pick up pace.

The bubble economy expanded so rapidly that the real economy could not support it, eventually leading to collapse. Since the 1990s, the entire economy has fallen into a long-term chronic depression and has failed to truly escape this difficult situation.

Section 13   Evidence from South Korea

South Korea is representative of industrial nations emerging rapidly after the war – known as one of The Four Asian Tigers. In terms of economic development conditions, as a peninsula country, South Korea has poor natural resources and a very weak economic foundation; this is very similar to Japan. South Korea implements an export-oriented development strategy, and relies on the support of foreign economies such as the US and Japan, in addition to strong governmental support. This is also similar to Japan.

In general, South Korea's economic development process is reflected in the continuous increase in industrial share and the relative decline of agriculture and even services. The economic growth rate stayed relatively high when the share of industry increased, as shown in Figure 5.7. It is clear that during this stage, industrial growth was the fundamental driving force of economic and social development.

South Korea began economic construction after the end of the Korean War in the mid-1950s. In view of small territory, lack of natural sources, and shortage of capital and technology, the country established an export-oriented strategy based on

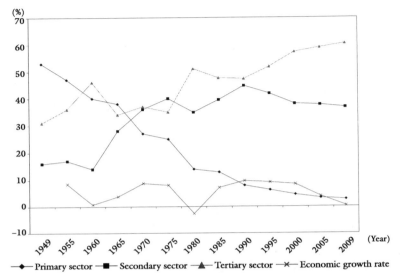

Figure 5.7 Economic Growth and Industrial Structure in South Korea
Source: Data before 1990 came from the Bank of Japan, *International Comparative Statistics*, data after 1995 came from the World Bank website, http://databank.worldbank. org/ddp/home.do?Step=12&id=4&CNO=2.

the international market. It took advantage of cheap domestic labor to develop labor-intensive industries. In the early 1960s, the government further prioritized economic development. Under "export first" and "trade centered" objectives, South Korea actively implemented an export-oriented policy: textiles saw tremendous progress, with 70% of products sold abroad. After the 1970s, steel, automobile, shipbuilding and machinery manufacturing gradually grew, significantly driving up the industrial share. In the 1990s, due to technology maturity and intensified international market competition, the share of industry increased slowly, and even began to decline, whereas the share of services rebounded to a certain extent. This situation weakened industrial contribution and more generally the national economy. When financial turmoil swept across Southeast Asia in 1997/98, South Korea was badly affected, suffering a sharp decline in the value of its currency and the Korean economy. These changes were thought-provoking.

Section 14   Evidence from Singapore

Singapore is an island nation. It was reduced to a British colony in 1842 and invaded by Japan a century later in 1942, three years after which Britain regained colonial rule. It officially became independent in August 1965, two years after merging with Malaysia. That being so, Singapore has a short history of economic development, which relies on the support of the international market. On the whole, economic progress has reflected the important role of industry in the national economy in an open market.

Singapore has a small territory, limited natural resources and a weak industrial base. It takes advantage of its geographical location to engage in re-export trade. When it was an autonomous state in 1959, this accounted for 80.8% of GDP. In the 1960s, Singapore began to implement an import substitution strategy centering on labor-intensive industries such as textiles, clothing, food and wood processing, which improved the employment and economic situation to some extent. In the 1970s, these labor-intensive industries began to enter the international market, and with strong government support, increased their market share annually. Simultaneously, the import substitution strategy was extended to capital-intensive industries, focusing on heavy industry such as shipbuilding and oil refining. With respect to services, Singapore vigorously developed the maritime industry and ocean business by creating favorable conditions to attract foreign ships to register and pay taxes. In the mid-1970s, the aforementioned sectors began to sell abroad and gradually became the nation's main exporters. Along with rapid industrial progress, the share of industry rose quickly; during this period, economic growth maintained a relatively rapid rate.

However, with aging technology, increasing labor costs, and the intensification of international market competition – especially the rise of trade protectionism – Singapore's economy was seriously challenged. After the United States removed Singapore from the generalized system of preferences (GSP) in 1984, industry was hit hard, with its share falling, and the economic growth rate also became negative. Singapore was forced to adjust its industrial structure. On the one hand, efforts were made to develop hi-tech industries to address the economic gap. On the other hand, focus was shifted to services such as foreign trade, transportation, finance and insurance, tourism, and international services. However, on the whole, hi-tech industries were still immature, and services depended entirely on the development of industry (and mainly foreign industrial sectors). As the foundation for economic growth was greatly weakened,

Table 5.6   Industrial Structure and Economic Growth in Singapore

Unit: S$ billion, %

Year	GDP	Proportion of agricultural sector	Proportion of industrial sector	Proportion of service sector	GDP growth rate
1973	17.02	1.6	40.1	58.3	–
1975	18.89	1.4	38.6	60.0	4.0
1978	23.69	1.3	39.2	59.5	8.6
1980	28.39	1.1	40.4	58.5	9.7
1983	35.96	0.8	40.7	58.5	8.2
1985	38.24	0.7	38.2	61.1	–1.8
1988	47.38	0.4	38.2	61.4	11.2
1990	56.26	0.3	38.0	61.7	8.7
1993	69.96	0.2	37.9	61.9	9.9

Note: GDP growth rate is the ratio of GDP of the current year to that of the previous year.
Source: International Bureau of the Bank of Japan, *International Comparative Statistics.*

Singapore's economic growth rate exhibited a downward trend, as shown in Table 5.6.

Section 15   Evidence from Thailand

Located in the middle of the Indochina, Thailand has a coastline of 2,600 kilometers in the south. The alluvial plain lying in the nation's center serves as the main area for agricultural

Table 5.7 Industrial Structure and Economic Growth in Thailand

Unit: billion baht, %

Year	GDP	Proportion of agricultural sector	Proportion of industrial sector	Proportion of service sector	GDP growth rate
1973	541.1	23.0	26.4	50.6	–
1975	592.7	22.5	26.5	51.0	4.9
1978	781.8	20.8	29.8	49.4	10.4
1980	862.5	18.9	29.9	51.2	5.0
1983	1014.8	18.4	31.6	50.0	5.5
1985	1123.4	18.1	31.3	50.6	4.7
1988	1472.6	15.3	34.3	50.4	13.3
1990	1845.9	12.9	37.4	49.7	11.8
1993	232.5	11.2	40.8	48.0	7.8

Note: GDP growth rate is the ratio of GDP of the current year to that of the previous year.
Source: International Bureau of the Bank of Japan, *International Comparative Statistics*.

production; it has become the key pillar of the national economy. Economic construction and industrialization began in earnest after Thailand recovered lost land following Japanese surrender in 1945. The share of industry continued to rise, driving rapid national economic development. As shown in Table 5.7, there is an inseparable relationship between the share of industry and economic growth.

Thailand was a typical agricultural country at the beginning of the war. By 1960, agriculture still accounted for 84% of the entire labor force, although the government devoted great energy to industrial development. In order to modernize, an economic development strategy prioritizing heavy chemical industry was formulated. However, this did not succeed due to weak industrial foundation, poor social infrastructure, and serious fund shortages. Instead, agriculture was severely hit, greatly impairing economic efficiency. At the same time, Thailand was burdened with huge foreign debt: debt servicing made up as much as 20% of annual revenue.

In view of this, a new strategy was adopted: accordingly, Thailand began to develop industrial sectors suited to domestic resources and labor, and pursued prosperity through agriculture, aquaculture, and livestock production. Simultaneously, the investment environment was improved, catalyzing rapid development in processing and labor-intensive industries, such as aquatic products, livestock, fruits, wooden furniture, clothing, and footwear. Then, taking advantage of currency appreciation in Japan and the Four Asian Tigers, Thailand absorbed some of the technology-intensive industries while expanding exports. This stimulated the quick and stable development of the entire economy.

In terms of industrial structure, industry gradually rose to occupy a central and leading role in the national economy. From 1970 to 1980, the average annual growth rate was 10%, nearly double that of agriculture. This tendency did not change in the 1980s: manufacturing expanded even more rapidly, with an average annual growth rate of 10.6% from 1970–1980 and 8.9% from 1980–1990. Other fast-growing industries included agricultural product processing, textiles, automobiles, and electronics.

Propelled by industry, Thailand maintained relatively fast economic growth. When industry slowed down in the mid-1980s, Thailand's economic growth rate also declined. This adds further evidence that traditional agricultural countries can achieve rapid growth only with the support of a fast-growing industrial sector.

Section 16 Evidence from India

Located in the center of the South Asian subcontinent, India ranks seventh globally in terms of territory and second in terms of population. In 1991, the population numbered 844 million. India faces the sea on two sides and has many rivers and lakes. Forests cover about 23% of the land area; farmland accounts for more than 50%, reaching 173 million hectares – the largest in Asia. This is extremely beneficial to agricultural production. India is rich in minerals, ranking amongst the top in the world by reserves of coal, iron, manganese, titanium, plating, thorium, monazite, mica and dolomite. There are also abundant oil, natural gas, bauxite, copper, gold, lead and zinc resources as well as water. These natural resources have provided relatively superior conditions for India's economic development.

The nation began industrialization after ending British colonial rule – becoming independent in March 1947. By implementing the Five-Year Plan, the Indian government leveraged foreign technology and capital to vigorously develop the public and mixed economy, establishing a relatively complete economic system. In this post-war process of economic development, the industrial share rose while agriculture continued to decline. However, the industrial share did not surpass agriculture until the early 1990s. Therefore, it is more appropriate to focus on this period when examining the role of industry in driving the national economy, as shown in Table 5.8.

Table 5.8   Industrial Structure and Economic Growth in India

Unit: billion rupees, %

Year	GDP	Proportion of agricultural sector	Proportion of industrial sector	Proportion of service sector	GDP growth rate
1973	1814.3	38.3	21.8	39.9	–
1975	2005.6	38.5	21.2	40.3	9.2
1978	2313.5	35.4	23.2	41.4	5.8
1980	2337.3	34.5	23.0	42.5	6.7
1983	2775.5	33.7	23.9	42.4	7.4
1985	3034.2	30.9	24.2	44.9	5.4
1988	3663.6	29.3	25.0	45.7	10.0
1990	4107.7	27.6	26.2	46.2	5.2
1993	4449.6	26.7	25.3	48.0	2.8

Note: GDP growth rate is the ratio of GDP of the current year to that of the previous year.
Source: International Bureau of the Bank of Japan, *International Comparative Statistics.*

Section 17 Evidence from Malaysia

Malaysia has reserves of tin, oil, natural gas, uranium, nickel, manganese, copper and bauxite – of which tin, oil and natural gas reserves represent a relatively high share of the world market.

Before independence in 1957, Malaysia was ruled and plundered by colonists and invaders. Afterwards, the nation developed its own economy and maintained high annual economic growth by relying on international capital and government support. Annual GDP growth was 6.5% from 1960 to 1970, 7.8% from 1970 to 1980, and 5.2% from 1980 to 1990. In terms of industrial structure, the industry share kept increasing, as shown in Table 5.9. This verifies the central role of the industry.

Malaysia's economic growth is mainly driven by the industrial sector. Initially, primary processing industries using natural resources as raw materials dominated the economy. Examples were labor-intensive and capital-intensive industries such as rubber, petrochemicals, metal smelting, wood processing, and textiles. The entire economic structure was affected by this model. By the late 1970s, the nation had still failed to update its economic structure: in 1979, primary products took up as much as 82% of total exports, yet because of great price fluctuations, Malaysia was relatively disadvantaged in international competition.

In view of this, a focus on channeling foreign investment to manufacturing was pursued in the 1980s; the government not only improved the soft environment for investment, but also vigorously advanced infrastructure construction such as hydropower, transportation and communication. Political and currency stability, high-quality labor, and low prices also contributed to the rapid increase in foreign capital inflow. As such, Malaysia was able to adjust its industrial structure, transferring labor-intensive industries to countries/regions with lower wage costs while striving to promote the development of relatively technology-intensive industries, such as, electronics and automobiles. In 1988, the automotive industry had an annual production capacity of 170,000 vehicles and exported to the United States and Britain. The electronics industry developed

Table 5.9   Industrial Structure and Economic Growth in Malaysia

Unit: billion gilts, %

Year	GDP	Proportion of agricultural sector	Proportion of industrial sector	Proportion of service sector	GDP growth rate
1973	27.06	29.0	33.3	37.7	–
1975	29.55	27.6	32.0	40.4	0.8
1978	37.89	25.1	34.8	40.1	6.7
1980	44.51	22.9	35.8	41.3	7.4
1983	53.58	21.1	36.3	42.6	6.2
1985	57.09	27.8	36.7	35.5	–1.1
1988	66.30	21.0	39.7	39.3	8.9
1990	79.45	18.6	42.1	39.3	9.7
1993	100.95	15.7	44.0	40.3	8.5

Note: GDP growth rate is the ratio of GDP of the current year to that of the previous year.
Source: International Bureau of the Bank of Japan, *International Comparative Statistics*.

more rapidly. In the late 1980s, Malaysia became the third largest semiconductor producer after Japan and the US, and the world's largest semiconductor exporter.

It is precisely because of rapid industrial progress that the Malaysian economy can maintain a relatively high growth rate. The negative economic growth in 1985 was caused by the decline industrial share. This reveals the negative aspect of relying on industry as the decisive force for socio-economic growth, as shown in Table 5.9.

Section 18   Evidence from the Philippines

The Philippines is an archipelago rich in fine harbors and mineral resources. From the mid-16th century until 1898, it was ruled by Spain. After this, it was governed by the US before it became officially independent in July 1946. The economic growth since the 1950s has clearly reflected the close relationship with industrial structure evolution, that is, fast economic growth accompanied by a rapid increase in industrial share; conversely, national economic growth becomes slower or even negative when industry slows or declines.

Industry made strides in the 1950s and 60s, owing to the successful implementation of an import substitution development strategy throughout the 50s. In terms of economic growth, the annual GDP growth rate stayed above 7%, and per capita GDP was second only to Japan in Asia. In the 1960s, due to policy failures and discontinuity, industry gradually slowed down. Under the impact of the two oil crises in the early 70s, both the domestic and international environment for economic development deteriorated, and the annual GDP growth rate shrank and fluctuated. In the mid-to-late 1970s and after, the Marcos government borrowed foreign debt to build more than 20 capital-intensive large-scale engineering projects targeting the domestic market, while neglecting to support industrial exports. These capital-intensive projects had high costs and low benefits, and survived on the state's monopoly. They weakened domestic purchasing power and failed to penetrate the international market. As traditional export industries lost strong policy support, the international balance of payments deficit expanded, and the domestic economy slumped – there was negative growth for three years from 1984 to 1986.

After coming to power in 1986, Aquino adopted a series of adjustment and reform measures, which targeted agricultural development and labor-intensive industries. He supported the export of manufactured goods and labor services, and simultaneously implemented a range of policies that covered land reform, privatization, interest rate increase, tax reform, deferred payment of foreign debts, foreign investment, and export processing zones. Consequently, industry rebounded and economic growth began to pick up. Nevertheless, many investors were discouraged by the political turmoil, heavy debt, and underdeveloped market economy; thus, the industrial sector and economic growth rate exhibited a downward trend in the 1990s, which severely undermined the country's growth potential and economic foundation, as shown in Table 5.10.

Table 5.10 Industrial Structure and Economic Growth in the Philippines

Unit: billion pesos, %

Year	GDP	Proportion of agricultural sector	Proportion of industrial sector	Proportion of service sector	GDP growth rate
1973	115.29	10.4	35.3	54.3	–
1975	129.25	9.7	35.5	54.8	5.7
1978	150.52	9.6	36.3	54.1	8.2
1980	178.22	8.5	37.4	54.1	8.4
1983	184.55	8.7	35.1	56.2	4.2
1985	196.59	8.7	36.2	55.1	2.7
1988	195.26	8.3	36.4	55.3	1.0
1990	210.54	8.0	37.6	54.4	4.2
1993	225.63	7.6	37.3	55.1	0.4

Note: GDP growth rate is the ratio of GDP of the current year to that of the previous year.
Source: International Bureau of the Bank of Japan, *International Comparative Statistics*.

Section 19 Evidence from Australia

Australia has rich natural resources and fishery resources across its vast territory. As early as the colonial period, from 1788 to 1900, it was dominated by agriculture and mining. By WWII, the situation was not fundamentally any different, although industry had made certain progress. Only after the war did industry develop rapidly enough to bring about major change to the economic structure.

During the 1950s and 60s, Australia actively promoted industrial production, which contributed to the rapid development of the manufacturing, mining, construction and service sectors. In the early 1980s, the country suffered a severe recession as a result of a major drought and sluggish international market demand. In face of this, the government began to implement economic reforms in 1983, including adjusting industrial structure, changing exchange rate policies, relaxing credit controls, lifting foreign exchange controls, and reducing

Table 5.11   Industrial Structure and Economic Growth in Australia

Unit: billion AU$, %

Year	GDP	Proportion of agricultural sector	Proportion of industrial sector	Proportion of service sector	GDP growth rate
1973	202.42	4.8	35.5	59.7	–
1975	208.14	5.1	34.7	60.2	2.8
1978	225.45	5.6	34.0	60.4	5.3
1980	238.59	4.1	34.6	61.3	3.0
1983	254.61	5.0	31.7	63.3	6.6
1985	277.21	4.5	32.4	63.1	3.7
1988	312.25	4.0	32.2	63.8	4.4
1990	319.47	4.5	31.3	64.2	–0.6
1993	334.50	–	–	–	4.2

Note: GDP growth rate is the ratio of GDP of the current year to that of the previous year.
Source: International Bureau of the Bank of Japan, *International Comparative Statistics*.

tariffs. These favorable factors improved trade conditions. Manufacturing labor productivity increased rapidly – at twice the growth rate of the entire economy. As shown in Table 5.11, the changes in industrial share explains the internal mechanism of Australia's economic growth to a certain extent.

Section 20   Evidence from China

I.   *Industrial Structure and Economic Growth*

Since reform and opening up, China has realized rapid economic growth driven by the speedy development of the secondary industry, in sharp contrast to the economic recession of service-centered countries during the same period.

Specific to stages, the average annual GDP growth rate was 7.84% from 1976–1980, 10.72% from 1981–1985, 7.9% from 1986–1990, 11.8% from 1991–1995, 10.29% from 1995–2000, 13.26% from 2000–2005, and 16.57% from 2000–2005.

In this process, the primary industry share rose from 28.37 to 30.40% from 1978–1980 and fell to 28.38% in 1990. As for secondary industry, its share increased marginally from 48.63 to 49.04% from 1978–1980, dropped to 43.65% in 1990, and rebounded to 48.80% in 1995 and further to 50.2% in 2000 before narrowing to 46.34% in 2010. The tertiary industry share decreased from 23 to 20.56% from 1978–1980 and then climbed all the way to 43.43% in 2009, as shown in Figure 5.8.[8]

China economically lags far behind developed countries such as the US and Japan. Nevertheless, it also exhibits a tendency

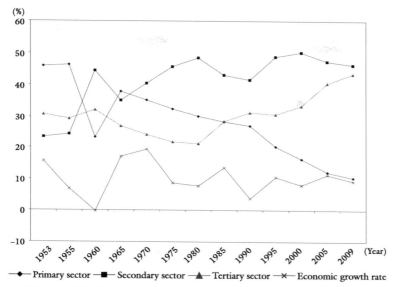

Figure 5.8 Economic Growth and Industrial Structure in China

Source: The data before 2000 are from the China Statistical Yearbook; the data after 2005 are from the World Bank website.
http://data-bank. Worldbank.org/ddp/home.do? Step=12&id =4&CNO=2.

for secondary industry to stimulate economic growth directly. Especially after 1985, a positive relation became more apparent as an unbalanced industrial structure featuring a low tertiary industry share was adjusted.

II. *Empirical Analysis on the Decisive Role of the Industrial Sector*

There is a lot of research on the evolution of industrial structure in China's economic growth. Therefore, this book will not go into details. This study intends, through the simplest

151

quantitative analysis, to empirically examine the relationship between economic growth and industry in China, in order to confirm that the industrial sector plays a decisive role in current society. A comparative analysis of China and the United States is also included out of academic rigor. This can further prove that economic growth in the US is still determined by industry, not services, though the service sector takes up an increasing proportion; also, economic and social development is still in the industrial stage, not the post-industrial stage.

As the complete and continuous sample data for panel analysis are unavailable due to data limitations, a simple quantitative analysis is conducted with the United States and China as cases to examine the relationship between sector-specific contribution and economic growth rates.

1. From the perspective of contribution rate, industrial sector growth is basically synchronized with economic growth. The contribution rate is often used to measure the contribution of an industry or sector to economic growth – the ratio of added value of each industry to GDP.

Assuming that $d_t^{(i)}$ is the contribution rate of industry i in year t; y_t is the GDP in year t; g_t is the GDP growth rate (economic growth rate) in year t; $y_t^{(i)}$ is the added value of industry i in year t; $g_t^{(i)}$ is the growth rate of industry i in year t; $w_t^{(i)}$ is the share of industry i in year t, then the formula to count the contribution rates of the three industries is as follows.

$$d_t^{(i)} = \frac{y_t^{(i)} - y_{t-1}^{(i)}}{y_t - y_{t-1}}$$

It can be expressed as follows:

$$d_t^{(i)} = \frac{w_{t-1}^{(i)} g_t^{(i)}}{w_{t-1}^{(1)} g_t^{(1)} + w_{t-1}^{(2)} g_t^{(2)} + w_{t-1}^{(3)} g_t^{(3)}} = \frac{w_{t-1}^{(i)} g_t^{(i)}}{g_t}$$

Based on the characteristics of data available, the formula can be written as follows:

$$d_t^{(i)} = w_t^{(i)} + \frac{w_t^{(i)} - w_{t-1}^{(i)}}{g_t}$$

Hence, the contribution rates of the three industries can be calculated. Long-term results are shown in Figures 5.9 and 5.10 respectively. With respect to the United States, the economic growth rate has fluctuated synchronously with the contribution

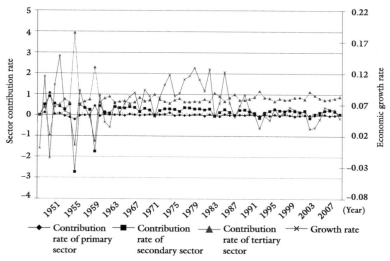

Figure 5.9 Relationship between the Economic Growth Rate and Sector-specific Contribution Rate in the United States

Source: US Department of Commerce website.

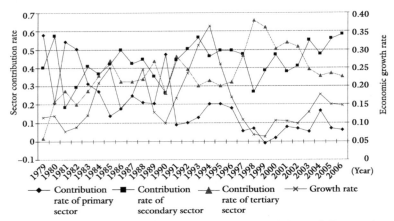

Figure 5.10   Relationship between the Economic Growth Rate and Sector-specific Contribution Rate in China

Source: China Statistical Yearbook.

rate of the secondary industry since the early 1950s (post war era). With respect to China, the contribution rate of secondary industry has shown characteristics related to economic growth fluctuations since reform and opening up in 1978. It is evident that a positive correlation exists between fluctuations in the contribution rate of secondary industry and economic growth rate in both countries. This further empirically explains how secondary industry provides the main driving force for economic growth.

2. From the perspective of correlation, the contribution rate of the industrial sector is positively correlated to the economic

growth rate, while the contribution rate of the service sector is negatively correlated.

In order to further study the relationship between economic growth and industrial structure of the two countries, the correlation analysis of some variables is introduced. The correlation coefficients r_{11}, r_{12}, r_{13} are calculated, which represent the contribution rate of the primary (CR11), secondary (CR12) and tertiary (CR13) industries to GDP growth rate (GDPRATE1) respectively. The value range is $[-1, 1]$.

Positive value indicates positive correlation, while negative value indicates negative correlation. A value equal or close to zero means the two variables show irregular changes and have no certain correlation. Assuming that x is the contribution rate of an industry; y is GDP growth rate; r_{1j} is the coefficient of correlation between GDP growth rate and added value of industry j at current price; r_{2j} is the correlation coefficient between GDP growth rate and the added value of industry j with inflation deducted, $j = 1$, 2, 3; then the formula to calculate the correlation coefficient r can be expressed as follows:

$$r = \frac{\Sigma (x - \bar{x}) (y - \bar{y})}{\sqrt{\Sigma (x - \bar{x})^2 \Sigma (y - \bar{y})^2}}$$

First, let us investigate the relationship between economic growth and industrial structure in the United States. Using data from 1948–2007, the contribution rates of the primary (CR11), secondary (CR12) and tertiary (CR13) industries and the GDP growth rate (GDPRATE1) are calculated at current price. The correlation coefficients r_{11}, r_{12} and r_{13} are obtained with the help of the SAS software. The results are as follows:

$$r_{11} = -0.22985, \qquad r_{12} = 0.44007, \qquad r_{13} = -0.32968$$

In the same way, calculations are also performed at chain price based on the 1948–2007 data. The results are as follows:

$$r_{21} = -0.25710, \qquad r_{22} = 0.45885, \qquad r_{23} = -0.35289$$

The results indicate that in the US, GDP growth correlates significantly positively with the contribution rate of secondary industry, but negatively correlates with the contribution rates of the primary and tertiary industries. In other words, although the tertiary industry dominates the industrial structure in absolute value, the secondary industry contributes most to economic growth. The secondary industry plays a positive role in promoting economic growth, while the primary and tertiary industries have negative effects.

Second, let us take a look at the relationship between economic growth and industrial structure in China. Based on the data from 1978–2006 of the primary, secondary, and tertiary industries, the results are as follows:

$$r_{11} = -0,11474, \qquad r_{12} = 0.43420, \qquad r_{13} = -0.18901$$

It is clear in this case that the GDP growth rate has a positive correlation with the contribution rate of secondary industry, but a negative correlation with the primary and tertiary industries. The results also prove the theoretical hypotheses raised earlier. The difference is that China's tertiary industry has been less developed for a long time, which restricts overall economic growth. As its progress has a positive effect on secondary industry, its side effect on economic growth is much smaller than the US.

Finally, quantitative analysis further proves the historical limitations of traditional theories on industrial structure. Based on empirical analysis, preliminary conclusions can be drawn – the rapid development of the second industry is positively correlated with economic growth rates, which is contrary to the tertiary industry. In other words, after an economy enters an industrial stage, the secondary industry will gradually rise as the leading contributor to economic growth. The cases of the United States, the world's largest economy claiming to have entered a "post-industrial society," and China, the world's second largest economy in the midst of industrialization, all prove the driving force for economic growth comes mostly from secondary industry.

Notes

1. Industrial structure: data of 1869–1937 from US Department of Commerce, *Historical Statistics of the United States (Volume 1)*, trans. Saito et al. (Hara Shobo, 1987), 240; data of 1940–1975 from B. Michelle MacMillan, *International Historical Statistics III – North and South Americas·Oceania (Japanese version)*, trans. Saito et al. (Hara Shobo, 1985), 911, 918; data of 1980–2000 from U.S. Department of Commerce, Bureau of Economic Analysis, Survey of Current Business (http://www.bea.doc. gov). Economic growth rate: data of 1869–1910 calculated according to B. Michelle MacMillan, *International Historical Statistics III – North and South Americas·Oceania (Japanese version)*, trans. Saito et al. (Hara Shobo, 1985). (compared with the previous year, the price of 1929); the data of 1910–1913 and 1929–1937 were the average values of their respective periods, and those of 1940–1970 were the ratio to the previous year, from

B. Michelle MacMillan, *International Historical Statistics III – North and South Americas-Oceania (Japanese version)*, trans. Saito et al. (Hara Shobo, 1985), 227; data of 1975 were the ratio to the previous year, from B. Michelle MacMillan, *International Historical Statistics III – North and South Americas-Oceania (Japanese version)*, trans. Saito et al. (Hara Shobo, 1985), 897; data of 1980–2000 from U. S. Department of Commerce, Bureau of Economic Analysis, Survey of Current Business (http://www.bea.doc.gov). The industrial structure and growth rate data since 2000 were from the World Bank website, http://datahank.worldbank.org/ddp/home.do?Step=12&id=4&CNO=2.

2. Data before 1975 from B. Michelle MacMillan, *International Historical Statistics I – Europe (1750–1975) (Japanese version)*, trans. Hiroshi Nakamura (Hara Shobo, 1986), 818, 826, 836, 841, 845, 856; Data since 1980 from the World Bank website, http://databank.worldbank.org/ddp/home.do?Step=12&id=4&CNO=2.

3. Data before 1975 from B. Michelle MacMillan, *International Historical Statistics I – Europe (1750–1975) (Japanese version)*, trans. Hiroshi Nakamura (Hara Shobo, 1986), 817, 821, 829, 840, 843, 849; data of 1980–1995 from Bank of Japan, *International Comparative Statistics (Japanese version)* (Bank of Japan International Bureau, 1997), 35–36. Data of 1950–1990 from German Federal Republic. Data since 2000 from the World Bank website, http://databank.Worldbank.org/ddp/home.do?Step=12&id=4&CNO=2.

4. Data before 1975 from B. Michelle MacMillan, *International Historical Statistics I – Europe (1750–1975) (Japanese version)*, trans. Hiroshi Nakamura (Hara Shobo, 1986), 817, 823, 831, 840, 844, 852; data of 1980–1995 from Bank of Japan, *International Comparative Statistics (Japanese version)* (Bank of Japan International Bureau, 1997), 35–36; Data since 2000 from the World Bank website, http://datahank.worldhank.org/ddp/home.do?Step=12&id=4&CN0=2.

5. Data before 1975 from B. Michelle MacMillan, *International Historical Statistics I – Europe (1750–1975) (Japanese version)*, trans. Hiroshi Nakamura (Hara Shobo, 1986), 821, 829, 842, 849; data of 1980–1995 from Bank of Japan, *International Comparative Statistics (Japanese*

version) (Bank of Japan International Bureau, 1997); Data since 2000 from the World Bank website, http://databank.worldbank.org/ddp/hime. do?Step=12&id=4&CNO=2.

6. Data before 1975 from B. Michelle MacMillan, *International Historical Statistics II – Japan·Asia·Africa (Japanese version)*, trans. Beicun Fu (Hara Shobo, 1986), 738, 739, 745; data of 1980–1990 from Japan Economic Planning Agency, **Annual Report on National Economic Accounting** *(Japanese version)* (Institute of Economic Research of Economic Planning Agency, 1997); data of 1995–2000 from web database of Japan Economic Planning Agency. Economic growth rate: data of 1985–1940 calculated according to *Long-term Economic Statistics* edited by Kazushi Okawa et al.; data of 1945–1970 from B. Michelle MacMillan, *International Historical Statistics II – Japan·Asia·Africa (Japanese version)*, trans. Beicun Shang (Hara Shobo, 1986), 728, 732; data of 1980–1990 from **Annual Report on National Economic Accounting** prepared by Japan Economic Planning Agency; data of 1995–2000 from web database of Japan Economic Planning Agency; data since 2005 from the World Bank website, http:// databank.worldbank.org/ddp/home.do?Step=12&id=4&CNO=2.

7. Data before 1975 from B. Michelle MacMillan, *International Historical Statistics II –Japan·Asia·Africa (Japanese version)*, trans. Beicun Fu (Hara Shobo, 1986), 738, 739, 745; data of 1980–1990 from Japan Economic Planning Agency, **Annual Report on National Economic Accounting** *(Japanese version)* (Institute of Economic Research of Economic Planning Agency, 1997); data of 1995–2000 from web database of Japan Economic Planning Agency. Economic growth rate: data of 1985–1940 calculated according to *Long-term Economic Statistics* edited by Kazushi Okawa et al.; data of 1945–1970 from B. Michelle MacMillan, *International Historical Statistics II – Japan·Asia·Africa (Japanese version)*, trans. Beicun Shang (Hara Shobo, 1986), 728, 732; data of 1980–1990 from **Annual Report on National Economic Accounting** prepared by Japan Economic Planning Agency; data of 1995–2000 from web database of Japan Economic Planning Agency; data since 2005 from the World Bank website, http:// databank.worldbank.org/ddp/home.do?Step=12&id=4&CNO=2.

8. According to the *China Statistical Yearbook* and data of the World Bank.

CHAPTER 6

Evidence from Reality:
Ill Effects of Servitization

For a long time, servitization, or post-industrialization, has been regarded as a general rule and prevailing trend. Servitization refers to the tendency of absolute advantage in services and their occupation of an ever-increasing share of national economy. On this account, Western economists believed – based on Clark's Law – that industrial society has become post-industrial.

However, as shown many times in earlier chapters, the increase in the share of the service sector is a temporary feature, usually appearing in a specific period within industrial society. It by no means represents a long-term and irreversible trend, let alone signals the emergence of a new society. This issue will be further illustrated by analyzing service sector expansion in the UK, the US, and Japan as well as the Asian financial crisis.

Section 1   Emergence and Essence of Servitization

I. *Emergence of Servitization*

As noted above, the share of the service sector increases in the process of economic development, but it does not denote an inevitable result in this. In a long economic growth cycle, the share of services keeps rising after surpassing industry. This phenomenon occurred only between the two industrial revolutions. On the one hand, such a rise is associated with the decline of industry and accompanied by the slowdown of economic growth, therefore, it is considered a consequence of economic recession. On the other hand, such a rise will be halted by the inevitable arrival of the new industrial revolution and industry re-growth.

However, servitization emerged, with long-term momentum, in many developed countries simultaneously after the 1970s. Although this process was accompanied by economic slowdown, there was no long-term negative growth. Noticing phenomena only, according to Clark's Law, Western economists wrongly deemed servitization as the development trend of the future, asserting that post-industrial society has arrived. Judging from reality from the 1970s onwards, the tendency of servitization is caused by many factors.

Firstly, servitization after the 1970s was a normal phenomenon following the climax of the Third Industrial Revolution. Examining the historical process of industrial revolution, the rapid economic development after WWII was a combined result of the Second and Third Industrial Revolutions. In the

Second Industrial Revolution in the early 20th century, the industrial system was effectively established by relying on the internal combustion engine, electric power, and petrochemical technologies from the First Industrial Revolution. However, this process was interrupted by the Great Depression of the 1930s and WWII. It was not until the post-war reconstruction of major capitalist countries that such a system was gradually established. Hence, post-war economic development was actually driven by achievements from the Second Industrial Revolution, plus technological innovation in a few industrial fields. As this process lasted until the 1970s, the industrial system was established and improved in these nations, showing signs of "maturation." Such a suspension of technological innovation would inevitably lead to a slowdown in industry growth; therefore, the rise in service share in developed countries is normal.

Secondly, the Third Industrial Revolution was not a complete industrial revolution. It concerned industrial innovation in certain fields such as microelectronics (and later information technology), nuclear energy, new materials, bioengineering and marine engineering. In fact, only microelectronics developed smoothly, driving household appliances and information technology (IT) industries. Other technological innovations have not been industrialized on a large scale, and nuclear energy technology has not been used for civilian purposes for many years due to its potential danger. In other words, despite the stagnation of technological innovation across much industry, small technological advances and innovations have constantly emerged in a few fields since the 1970s, giving rise to a stream of new sunrise industries. This leads to the servitization of the entire economic structure and a situation where "structural growth" in a few industries drives economic development. Some people notice the increase in service share while overlooking the long-term role of industry, or examine the absolute expansion of gross economic product without considering the long-term slowdown of economic growth. That being so, they wrongly deem servitization, which maintains slow economic growth, to represent the future direction of development.

Thirdly, the international transfer of industries has spurred the servitization of developed economies. Developed countries underwent fast economic growth from the end of WWII to the breakout of the oil crisis in the early 1970s. With the maturity of developed economies such as the United States, Japan, and those in Western Europe, traditional industries, such as textiles, and heavy chemicals were often transferred from developed countries to developing countries. This tendency generally began in the mid-1960s. By the early 1980s, new industrial economies in Asia had emerged, including South Korea, Singapore, Hong Kong and Taiwan – collectively known as the Four Asian Tigers.

To China, the international transfer of industry has become more significant after reform and opening up, which has played its part in the average annual growth rate of over 10% for more than three decades. At the same time, India, Thailand, and Vietnam also keep absorbing industries from foreign countries. In this context, the share of the industrial sector naturally diminishes in developed economies. Future scholars represented by Daniel Bell, from their own perspective, argued that a post-industrial society represents the future. They not only ignore the basic and dominant role of material production in economic activities, but also fail to take the global integration of economy, and the servitization of developed economies built on the industrialization of emerging economies, into account.

II. *Essence of Servitization*

The post-industrial society is not a new form of society that has excelled in industry. Its basic characteristics – the sharp decline of material production share (especially industry) and the constant increase of services – only occur in a specific historical period. It reflects the incapability of industrial technology, prior to qualitative changes, to solve the contradictions with production relations as well as material and spiritual needs. This essentially determines that the expansion of services is temporary and limited, and will, by no means, prevent or change the infinite development of industry.

Firstly, from the perspective of social needs, spiritual needs tend to expand rapidly while effective material needs become relatively saturated or even stagnant. However, spiritual needs are carried by material products. The services that people enjoy and the facilities and methods they use are all provided by material production, and the leisure time to enjoy services is also enabled by labor productivity improvement. Therefore, economic activity in services are confined to the scope allowed by material production (especially industry); this means the expansion of services is limited. By relying on the transformation of industrial technology, industry can advance without limit.

Secondly, from the perspective of productivity development, so-called post-industrialization brought about by the relative stagnation of industry and improvement of labor productivity in services is temporary. There are two reasons: i) The progress of science and technology and the revolution of industrial technology are unstoppable; and ii) The work efficiency of services can only be improved only within the technical capabilities of industry, and the economic and social impacts are partially positive, partially negative, and even partially fictitious.

On the one hand, industrial decline will fundamentally undermine service development. Since the 1970s, labor productivity in services has improved rapidly, and office automation has been gradually introduced, increasing excess profits. Simultaneously, a large number of employees have been squeezed out, reducing employment and exerting a negative impact on national income. These consequences fundamentally dampen consumer demand for services.

On the other hand, against the decline of material production, the expansion of services is bound to be partially fictitious. The physical parts of the service sector that directly serve production operate only as per the demand of material production; only those parts of the virtual economy, such as finance, securities, futures, and real estate, can break away from material production and expand without control. In reality, the inflation brought about by economic intervention, such as the issuance of public bonds, currencies, and reduction of interest rates, can directly enlarge the virtual economy; and land acquisition and unrealistic economic plans can artificially push up the price, encouraging rampant speculation. This has occurred in Japan and the United States. In short, the expansion of services alongside the expansion of the virtual economy does not suggest services have replaced the industry as the dominant force; it cannot even explain its own expansion in a true sense.

Thirdly, it is precisely because of the partially fictitious expansion that its contribution to economic growth is limited and temporary. Over a certain period, service growth may spur the development of the entire economy, but soon, the bubble will burst. A larger bubble produces more profound and lasting negative consequences. In the so-called post-industrial stage, the economic growth rate of major developed countries has plummeted, in sharp contrast with the fast growth period of industry. This has been illustrated by figures and tables on the relationship between industrial structure and economic growth in Chapter 5.

Finally, it should be noted that the expansion of services results from the expansion of material production in terms of connotation and extension. For connotation, the technological advance of material production drives the entire economy forward by increasing demand capacity and leisure. At the same time, it provides services with better equipment and tools to improve productivity. In terms of extension, some parts of material production continue to be divorced from the production process and become an independent, specialized sector. For instance, commerce that undertakes product realization and production material purchases, transportation that supports labor displacement, production materials and products, and education that improves labor quality, are all part of material production. Due to the narrow understanding of material production sectors today, these are now categorized in the service sector. In essence, however, it is the expansion of material production that constitutes the true expansion of services.

Section 2 Evidence from the British Economic Recession

As well as being one of the first nations to industrialize, the United Kingdom was amongst the victors of WWII, though it was still heavily affected by the war; it did not receive the same influx of resources as Japan and Germany during the post-war period.

Since then, British governments have all implemented Keynesian economic policies, yet the economy has been in a relative state of stagflation for several years. Though the aging of industrial technology has been alleviated to some extent, the UK has fallen behind Japan, Germany and the US in technological progress. Consequently, the servitization of the British economy started much earlier than in the US and Japan.

Britain's industrial sector stagnated and dwindled in the 1970s, while services developed rapidly – it rose at the same rate as industry fell. Economic growth picked up in the 1980s owning to vigorous support for industry. However, in general, economic recession has manifested since the 1950s. Economic growth was slow until the 1990s, presenting a typical "British disease."

In the aftermath of WWII, the successive implementation of Keynesian policies led to financial crisis and inflation. After coming to power in 1979, the Conservative Party, led by Margaret Thatcher, turned to monetarist economics, which reduced public utility expenditures and fiscal deficits, lowered inflation, and stimulated economic growth. Simultaneously, a series of policies were adopted to accelerate industrial restructuring. With this assistance, hi-tech industries such as IT developed rapidly, rendering an average annual growth rate of 18% since 1985. Such progress improved traditional industry competitiveness, and catalyzed a transformation. From 1982–88, average annual growth of GNP hit 3.6%, a record high since the war. In addition, the government turned fiscal deficits into surpluses: in 1990, the fiscal surplus reached 7 billion pounds, suggesting the national economy had improved to a certain degree.[1]

In the 1990s, much of Western Europe and Japan fell into depression. Despite good development momentum in the US economy, it was not enough to prop up the global economy alone. In the UK, economic growth began to slow again. Following the long-term decline of industry, the service sector also lost its support and vitality.

Section 3   Evidence from the US Economic Recession

Since its founding, the US economy has experienced two periods of rapid industrial development, embodied in the second and third industrial revolutions. Great progress was made in the midst of the Second Industrial Revolution, then the Great Depression broke out in the 1930s, followed by WWII. The US took advantage of high war demands for military equipment to galvanize industry and climb out of recession, entering the Third Industrial Revolution. Afterwards, the US experienced rapid economic growth driven by industry, before slipping into recession.

I.   *End of the Third Industrial Revolution*

Since the end of the war, average growth has taken a downward trend. The share of services has risen sharply; in contrast, both industrial and agricultural sectors have declined in the long run.

In the early 1960s, industry began declining. In the mid-60s, growth in labor productivity of manufacturing decreased year-on-year. The share of traditional light industry such as textiles, leather and clothing continued to fall by small margins; correspondingly, the share of services began to increase substantially. At the time, US services, especially finance and trade, remained strong enough to influence the world, and could take advantage of monopolies to secure a large share of industrial profits of various countries. Hence, on the whole, economic recession was not severe.

In the 1970s, the global economic system of the capitalist world, underpinned by the Bretton Woods system and the General Agreement on Tariffs and Trade (GATT), began to collapse. This, coupled with the oil crisis, plunged the US, and many other countries into recession. Among heavy industry, steel and shipbuilding showed signs of decline due to aging equipment and high costs; the automotive industry lost its international advantage as a result of ignoring the development of fuel efficiency. In addition, high wages and labor benefits pushed up production costs. Heavy chemicals were thereupon reduced to sunset industries, while many emerging industries, especially hi-tech, developed rapidly. Thereafter, industry suffered long-term depression due to the lack of revolutionary technology. In the 1980s, the industrial share of the economy began to drop sharply.

At this stage, the share of services increased substantially in terms of employment and output value. Meanwhile, the share of labor services in personal consumption expenditure was rising above 50%. Of course, this was related to the high inflation rate of services relative to other sectors. In foreign trade, revenues from transportation, communication, insurance, advertising and investment grew noticeably. Labor trade gradually raised its share and maintained a large surplus, which played an important role in reducing the balance of payments deficit. At the same time, services such as computer information processing, real estate, public relations, management consulting, and equipment leasing emerged in large numbers. The growth of services was attributed to improved labor productivity on the one hand, and to the expansion of spiritual needs relative to material needs on the other hand. Besides, financial allocations from the government supported the construction of entertainment and tourism facilities, and spurred investment in education and scientific research. A series of reforms carried out from the late 1970s, especially after Reagan took office, also injected great impetus to transportation, communication and financial industries.

In terms of industrial structure, from the 1950s to the 1990s, the service share remained high with growth momentum, while the industrial share declined. However, the entire economy fell into long-term recession during the same period. Economic growth in recent years driven by active industry once again indicates that services cannot be the focal point of a modern developed society; industry has an inherent connection with economic growth.

II. IT Revolution and Its Limitations

In the 1990s, the IT revolution arose in the United States. Since then, computer technologies and products have quickly arrived on the global market. The IT economy enabled US prosperity throughout the 1990s, but it did not change the economic tendency of servitization.

The IT industry encompasses IT machinery manufacturing and services. Despite prosperous development, it has not been deeply integrated with production activities of the entire industrial system, but rather has stimulated market vitality as a consumer product. New IT-based office machinery and word processing have successfully changed consumption structure: IT manufacturing mainly occurs in the United States and Japan, of which the US takes a dominant share of about 80%. In addition, software services have flourished with the application of IT machinery, contributing to long-term prosperity.

However, the servitization tendency has not changed in this process. Although IT machinery is highly priced and has a long service life, it falls into the category of durable consumer goods. After a period of popular market expansion, market growth slows down, adding pressure on prices and costs. With the increase of domestic production costs, IT machinery manufacturing began to shift to emerging economies in the 21st century. But conversely, the IT economy has made the US more aware of its primary position in the international division of labor. Entrepreneurs pay more attention to advanced technology and give up traditional industry, which accelerates the overseas transfer of traditional industry. In addition, information services such as software development (a continuation of IT development), continue to make strides, highlighting the economic tendency of servitization.

Besides, the prosperity of the IT economy in the US has not affected the status of heavy chemical industries. IT machinery application in the production field is mainly reflected in the penetration of industrial robots, which can increase production efficiency and precision, but do not change the core technologies. Cars manufactured with the help of industrial robots will not turn into airplanes, but can be more exquisite and of better quality. In other words, the IT boom is still unable to address the stagnation of core technologies from traditional production; this foreshadowed the subsequent subprime mortgage crisis.

III. Root Cause of the Subprime Mortgage Crisis

In reality, the US subprime mortgage crisis, as a consequence of recession of the real economy, ignited a global financial crisis. It proved that relying on the tertiary industry, especially the virtual economy, to pursue economic growth is inappropriate and even harmful. Financial crisis is essentially a manifestation of difficulties in the real economy. Since the 1970s, the secondary sector has been in decline while the real economy has grown slowly. Technology based on the second and third industrial revolutions has been aging. Although the IT revolution begun in the 1990s, IT only made heavy chemical industries precise, networked and convenient, without fundamentally changing it. The boom of information machinery and information services brought about by the IT revolution lasted only ten years. In the 21st century, the secondary sector worsened and the overall economy stagnated, resulting in insufficient effective demand. In view of this, American tycoons created financial bubbles through derivatives, which stimulated effective demand and realized massive demand ahead of time. However, since the real economy remained sluggish, such growth could not solve the problem, eventually leading to the subprime mortgage crisis.

Section 4   Evidence from Japan's Bubble Economy

In the 1970s, the Japanese economy began to show servitization tendencies. The industrial sector, especially manufacturing based on heavy chemicals, went into recession and was subject to adjustment. In pursuit of high-speed economic growth, the Japanese government adopted a series of fiscal and financial policies. However, as the industrial adjustment had not yet been completed, such fiscal and financial incentives were mainly absorbed by services, leading to a malignant expansion of the speculative economy.

Against this backdrop, industrial structure began to change. Statistically, industrial sector decline was not obvious, but a slower growth rate suggested the contribution of industry diminished considerably. When it comes to the internal mechanism of economic operation, the role of industry was greatly weakened, becoming even less than services.

Following the 1971 Nixon Shock, the growth rate of industrial and mining production fell to 1.9%. In view of this, the Japanese cabinet launched the Plan for Remodeling the Japanese Archipelago, which fueled speculation. Large companies competed to buy land in hope of profiting from price rises. A range of companies, including real estate, trading, construction, private railway, bank, and insurance firms, as well as textile and non-ferrous metal companies all joined the ranks of land purchasers. Financial institutions actively provided funds based on land accepted as collateral because land security enhanced significantly with land prices. Consequently, land prices soared throughout Japan, leading to rampant land and stock speculation, skyrocketing prices, and serious asset inflation. In response, the deposit reserve ratio was raised. Nevertheless, due to inflation, the interest rate was still relatively low, which further encouraged massive inflation. During this period, nominal GNP kept growing so rapidly that the Japanese government mistakenly believed its policies were effective. This paved the ground for the bubble economy that began in the late 1980s.

In October 1973, the oil crisis broke out. The growth of government public utilities slowed as the prices of basic supplies shot up. The force behind the rise in land prices was lost, putting an end to this dangerous expansion. Industrial and mining production shrank significantly, with the annual growth rate plunging to 9.7% (by today's standards this would be high but during that period the figure was normally around 15–20%). The oil crisis caused the rapid economic growth centered on heavy chemicals to stop. As the industrial sector shifted focus to internal adjustments, private investment in equipment grew more slowly and the economy entered a low-growth period.

Later, Japan's financial sector moved gradually towards liberalization and internationalization. With the introduction of a modern computer-centric office system, technological revolution was unleashed. Finance also became increasingly integrated with commerce: with the support of banks, the installment method was adopted in competitive sales; businesses had to rely on loans, especially during high inflation. Such long-term residential loans also contributed to soaring land prices in the subsequent bubble economy. In addition, economic activities were virtualized. Companies no longer needed a large amount of capital investment. Instead, they leveraged short-term liquidity by issuing corporate bonds to arbitrage in the current market. Individuals attached importance to the increase in interest income due to asset balance increases and economic slowdown.

In the early 1980s, the US economic recovery and higher real interest rates created favorable conditions for Japanese exports. From 1974 to 1985, Japan's real GDP registered an average annual growth rate of 4.3%, of which exports contributed as much as 35%; far more than 16% from 1965–1973 when annual economic growth was 9.4%. During this period, industry resumed its role of driving the economy forward, but trade frictions intensified.

Following the 1985 meeting of the Group of Five finance ministers, the Japanese yen appreciated rapidly. While service industries such as electricity and gas improved greatly, industrial exports were hit hard. The current account surplus expressed in US dollars widened significantly. At the same time, wholesale prices declined and retail prices remained stable, meaning the added value of enterprise increased. In 1986, industrial and mining productivity was only 0.2% lower than in 1985, but economic growth dropped to 2.9% from 4.8%. This once again demonstrates that the driving force of industry had weakened.

The international environment facing Japan severely deteriorated with the intensification of trade frictions and the surge in trade surplus. Under pressure from the international community, the nation was forced to pursue domestic demand-driven growth. To this end, the Japanese government launched a set of emergency economic measures from 1987 onwards, focusing on large-scale investment in public utilities, state housing loans, and tax reduction and compensation. The official interest rate was reduced to 2.5% in February 1987 and maintained until early 1989. These policies, coupled with increased actual consumption capacity and expanded consumer expectations brought about by the appreciation of the yen, contributed to the vicious expansion of the bubble economy – known as the Heisei Boom.

At this time, domestic demand was, to a considerable extent, virtual. In view of relative price stability, the Japanese government lost vigilance against inflation. It adopted an unnecessary low-interest-rate policy in response to currency appreciation, and a comprehensive fiscal policy to stimulate growth. As most of the manufactured products of heavy chemicals reached a state of saturation, the consumption of high-end brand-name products, cars, and houses expanded rapidly. Industry began to scale up equipment investment on the one hand, and expanded operations to other industries (for diversification) on the other hand, especially in real estate. This led to an unprecedented growth in capital demand; loan rate reductions created a good opportunity for industry, and banks were encouraged to lend to profitable real estate companies, non-financial banks, and personal consumers, since banking costs increased under the impact of financial liberalization. Consequently, land and stock prices shot up amidst speculations surges, and went beyond the normal range of prices. Subsequently, companies, individuals and banks all used land as collateral to borrow and lend money. Thus, the focus of economic development gradually shifted to inflated land speculation, stock speculation, corporate equipment investment, and individual aristocratic consumption – driven by house and investment borrowings secured by land and stock prices. Economic growth deviated from real growth in this scenario.

After tighter financial policies were adopted in 1989, all factors that once supported the rise of stock prices turned negative, removing the grounds for stock speculation. With the fall of stock prices, companies became financially strained. Finding it more difficult to obtain funds, they showed little enthusiasm for investment, driving down stock prices further. Land prices also declined after 1991. Noticing consumer expectations were severely dampened, investment in durable consumer goods and houses turned sluggish. Economic adjustment across the board began in 1992. Nevertheless, economic recovery was weak, despite many large-scale fiscal policies and ultra-low interest rates.

Section 5   Evidence from the Asian Financial Crisis

I. *Formation of the Crisis*

The Thai financial crisis in July 1997 quickly swept Southeast Asia and further spread to South Korea, Japan, and Russia, covering almost all East Asian countries and regions except mainland China. The impact of this crisis lingers on. In this sense, it is not limited to Southeast Asia, and should be viewed on a larger scale. Looking into the internal mechanism of the time, this crisis can be considered as the continuation and recurrence of Japan's bursting bubble from the early 1990s. It is an outcome of untimely development policies, imperfect financial management systems, and malignant expansion of the virtual economy in Southeast Asia, in addition to Japan's long-term economic depression and shrinking foreign direct investment (FDI).

Following Japan's depression, large multinational companies such as Toyota, Sony and Panasonic all scaled down FDI, especially long-term production capital. Many Southeast Asian countries relied on foreign capital, especially Japanese capital, to improve technology and support exports. The withdrawal of Japanese capital reduced supply to Southeast Asia. This forced countries in the region to use short-term capital with high liquidity and high risk – pushing the financial sector to the brink of instability.

In this context, financial crisis first broke out in Thailand in Autumn 1997. Since the 1980s, Thailand achieved rapid economic growth through the export processing industry, with cheap labor as its main resource. From 1985–95, average annual growth was around 10%. International trade accounted for 42% of its GDP in 1986 and 85% in 1996. Because of heavy reliance on the international market, the Thai economy was extremely vulnerable to global shocks, with no currency buffer from its fixed exchange rate system. Against a strong US dollar, the Thai baht was overvalued in exchange rate terms. Consequently, exports declined. Thailand's export growth rate plunged from 22.5% in 1995 to 3% in 1996; its current account deficit was huge, reaching $8 billion in 1994, $13.5 billion in 1995 and $16.2 billion in 1996. This represented 8.5% of its GNP, exceeding the internationally recognized red line of 5%.

To make up for the current account deficit, Thailand began to relax restrictions on foreign capital in 1992. The return of Hong Kong to China in 1997 fueled Bangkok's ambition to rival the city as an international financial center. In 1996, the net inflow of foreign capital was $18 billion. In May 1997, total foreign debt reached $90 billion, accounting for about 49% of GNP. This foreign capital flowed to the virtual economy, such as high-profit securities and real estate. This accelerated the decline of exports and boosted the excessive development of the bubble economy.

Thailand's economic growth slowed after 1996. The real estate sector fell into turmoil, creating a chain reaction in the financial sector. A government briefing in May 1997 on the bad export situation then sparked a wave of speculation. The Bank of Thailand used nearly $4 billion in foreign exchange reserves to stabilize the Thai baht. Even so, due to weak exports, limited foreign exchange reserves and economic slump, Thailand announced on July 2 that it would abandon the pegged exchange rate system – this ignited the financial crisis in Southeast Asia.

The International Monetary Fund (IMF), as well as some regional nations, pledged $16.7 billion in loans to Thailand, but this failed to prevent the spread of the crisis. Today, electronic and internationalized financial tools have made financial operations extremely conductive, proliferative and speculative. On October 1, 1997, the Thai baht had tumbled 32.6% compared to July 1. The Philippine peso, Indonesian rupiah, and Malaysian ringgit also fell by 25.1% to 27.8%. Simultaneously, stock prices in Southeast Asia plummeted, with the impact spreading to Latin

America. In the week before July 18, the stock prices of Brazil, Peru, and Argentina dropped by 14.99%, 6.47%, and 5.70% respectively.

This financial crisis also set off a chain reaction in Northeast Asia. South Korea saw its bubble economy burst, with a sharp currency depreciation putting the financial sector on the verge of collapse. Japan also suffered from the crisis. As the yen depreciated to 140:1 against the US dollar, economic recovery was far off. Russia also felt pressure from currency devaluation in the context of deepening reforms. Overall, this financial crisis had a severe effect on the world economy.

II. Analysis of the Contributions and Consequences of the Asian Financial Crisis

In the entire 20th century, the 1997 financial crisis is recognized by scholars at home and abroad to be second only to the financial crisis of 1929. Its negative impact has been so profound that many countries are still affected. Among these are Japan, South Korea and Singapore, and Thailand, Indonesia, Philippines, and Malaysia, which have developed rapidly in recent years. In fact, the outbreak heralded the end of the East Asian economic growth miracle. Where the financial storm swept, currencies plunged; interest rates rose; stock prices fell; bank runs occurred; and financial companies closed down one after another, dragging economies to the brink of collapse. To cope with this, nations have paid a heavy price: Thailand consumed $4 billion in foreign exchange reserves in May alone; Malaysia lost 200 billion ringgits, equivalent to the sum of the five-year budget; and

South Korea suffered a sharp drop of foreign exchange reserves, prompting citizens to provide relief by donating gold and silver jewelry. What's worse, the crisis dampened investor confidence. Subsequently, foreign capital withdrew. Since World Bank loans were completely inadequate, crisis-stricken countries found themselves with insufficient funds and weak economic drivers.

1. Ill effects from the malignant expansion of the bubble economy.

As noted earlier, economic structure was very unbalanced in Japan, South Korea and Southeast Asia at large. Financial crisis was caused by the uncontrolled expansion and final collapse of the tertiary industry, especially real estate and finance. This crisis underlined how vicious expansion of the virtual economy will inevitably produce serious consequences, regardless of economic growth and development.

In Japan, the virtual economy began expanding as early as the mid-1970s. However, influenced by traditional theories on industrial structure, successive Japanese governments regarded the large-scale development of secondary industry as a general trend. Without sufficient vigilance, they promoted land development and financial expansion, lowering interest rates several times to stimulate speculative activities. After the collapse of the bubble economy in the early 90s, such ingrained flaws have held off economic recovery.

South Korea has also experienced excessive development of the virtual economy. Following a long economic growth period, sufficient funds were no longer invested in industry. Instead, they flowed to real estate and securities that are highly profitable. In 1994, Asian stock markets were volatile: stock prices even declined 20% when US interest rates rose. Only in South Korea did stock prices keep rising.

Southeast Asian countries such as Thailand have the same problems. In recent years, a total of $230 billion in funds has been invested in Thai real estate. This not only creates a price bubble, but also results in oversupply. At present, about half the buildings are vacant, and most financial institutions are unable to repay foreign loans. Foreign investment that has become bad debt is estimated to reach about $20 billion. Similar problems exist in Indonesia, the Philippines and Malaysia.

Evidently, the uncontrollable expansion of the bubble economy does not mean the national economy has grown in a real sense. On the contrary, it manifests a serious imbalance of economic structure, leading to a hotbed of economic and financial crises.

2. A culture that seeks quick returns and instant benefits.

It is with strong government incentives that countries achieved rapid economic growth before the financial crisis. For developing and underdeveloped countries, a government-led model may be successful in propelling economic takeoff and accelerating construction. That being so, radical and arbitrary policies that do not consider the objective conditions or respect market rules may generate negative effects. Practice has proved that in recent years, unrealistic development desires and imperfect management systems have directly contributed to the financial crisis.

Firstly, forcibly pursuing unrealistic development visions is a common problem. For example, in the face of intensified competition and rising trade protectionism, South Korea carried on its export-oriented strategy by excessively opening-up capital markets. This attracted a lot of hot money to its securities industry. Although financial crisis broke out in Mexico at the end of the year, the South Korean government remained optimistic about its economic strength and continued to welcome foreign capital. Thailand was eager to develop quickly, and committed to open capital markets, partially, in a bid to replace Hong Kong as an Asian financial center. As mentioned earlier, the Thai government turned a deaf ear to the IMF crisis warning. These practices ultimately accelerated the crisis.

Secondly, flawed banking systems are also common in these countries. In terms of bank operations, crisis-stricken countries generally have Japanese-style over-lending problems. Because of policy interventions, banks take massive risks by granting huge loans to less efficient industrial sectors. This mechanism can be positive when growth momentum is relatively stable, but when the entire economy is dominated by the virtual economy, it will inevitably accelerate financial collapse. In addition, collusion between government and the banking system undermines the scientific quality of financial policies. For example, in South Korea, the financial system has always been subject to strict government regulation: bank governors and senior managers are all appointed by the government; bank loans are often manipulated behind the scenes by government officials and large companies, since banks cannot examine their financial risks. In Thailand, many leaders of the ruling and opposition parties have personal ties with financial companies and banks. For this reason, they ignored the warning signs and delayed reforms. Desperate efforts to save the Thai baht with billions of dollars failed to alleviate the situation, only increasing the final price.

Thirdly, exchange rate policies beyond the capabilities of Southeast Asian countries are also an important factor. These countries have implemented a pegged exchange rate system for a long time. In recent years, as the US dollar has strengthened, various currencies have appreciated to the point of overvaluation, creating room for depreciation. In fact, currency overvaluation has placed considerable resistance on economic growth in Southeast Asia, especially in exports. However, reform efforts from many regional countries were ineffective or non-existent.

Clearly, we still inhabit an industrial society; the main principles and mechanisms of economic development are still centered on industry. Government behavior can change the economic development process to a certain extent, but it cannot violate objective laws. Once divorced from the principles of the market mechanism, policies are at the mercy of political interests and subjective desires, and thus are doomed to fail.

3. The financial crisis reflects the limitations of export-oriented strategies.

The financial crisis reflects the dual nature of export-oriented economic development strategies adopted by Japan, South Korea, and Southeast Asian countries. Although such strategies offer an effective method for rapidly advancing industrialization, its success requires many complementary objective conditions, such as production cost advantages. Generally, less advanced or developing countries have no advantages in production technology, but most have relative advantages of cheap labor. However, labor prices are bound to rise with economic development. If costs cannot be reduced in a timely manner through technological advance, exports will encounter problems. Developing countries generally adopt an export-oriented development strategy that relies excessively on imports and exports. Thus, these economies are largely at the whims of the international market. Moreover, the countries that have lost their labor advantage will soon be challenged by newcomers.

Japan had to turn to domestic demand expansion when its export strategy was met with strong European and American protectionism, and fierce competition from exports of developing countries. In the process of expanding domestic demand, however, the development of new industrial technologies was ignored, and huge excess capital was invested in virtual economic sectors.

South Korea took advantage of Japan's foreign transfer of capital and technology in the 1980s to vigorously develop an export-oriented economy. Heavy external dependence of up to 40% made it difficult to maintain economic stability against a fluctuating international market. In 1995, the export growth rate was as high as 30.3%, but in 1996, it plunged to 3.8%. The current account deficit also surged from around $10 billion to $23.7 billion in these two years. In view of this, South Korea actively pushed for open capital markets in order to expand exports. It is this hasty move that led the nation into the same trap as Mexico.

The situation in Southeast Asia was even more grim. Pressure on current account balances had increased with labor costs. Without a flexible exchange rate system, it was impossible for these countries to automatically adjust such imbalances. Thus, exports were bound to shrink if production technology was not advanced sufficiently. The short-sighted push for virtual economy would inevitably undermine the economic foundation and trigger a financial crisis.

At present, the Northeast Asian economy is already in crisis: Japan, South Korea, and Russia have suffered greatly, and China is also facing tremendous pressure from currency devaluation. Simultaneously, the US and the EU maintain stable economic growth momentum. As described earlier, the Asian financial crisis is a double-edged sword: it provides many profound implications while ruthlessly preventing the spread of the bubble economy. From a short-term perspective, the financial crisis has caused huge damage. From a long-term perspective, the mandatory adjustments entailed will help these countries return to healthy and stable development. Surviving this severe test, these Asian economies will rely more firmly on the development of material production sectors. Governments will more soberly follow the laws of market economy in reform, and truly pay attention to the development of science and industrial technology.

Ultimately, we must recognize that we are still in an industrial society; the industrial sector still holds a central position in the national economy, providing the driving force of economic growth. The service sector, especially the virtual economy, grows along with the industrial sector. Its advanced development and uncontrollable expansion may render false prosperity for a while, but will eventually cause a serious imbalance, overheat, and induce financial crisis.

Notes

1. Institute of World Economics and Politics Chinese Academy of Social Sciences, Editorial Department of the Journal of World Economy, *A Contemporary Practical Compendium of World Economy* (Beijing: China Prices Press, 1994), 444.

CHAPTER 7

Thinking of Development

The relationship between industrial structure and economic growth is key for mankind to explore the laws of economic activities and economic development. The different understandings of this relationship will affect the thinking of decision makers, thereby changing the future of an economy. We note with regret that the United States, Japan, much of Asia, and even the whole world, are deeply troubled by excessive servitization, caused in part by blind admiration of the theoretical paradigm of post-industrial society – as represented by Clark's Law. Even in the present climate, the decade-long global financial crisis, ignited by the US subprime mortgage crisis in 2007/8, is still with us. The cruel economic reality has mercilessly demonstrated the limitations of

Clark's Law and reminded us that we should re-think the road ahead.

Section 1   The Power of the Times

Each theory is a product of specific historical circumstances and practice is the criterion for testing truth. With the passage of time, there will inevitably be phenomena in practice that cannot be explained by existing truths. While respecting the achievements of predecessors, we must never shy away from moving forward. Only by keeping pace with the times can we reflect on the limitations of traditional theories and create new ones.

I.   *Times and Theories*

Clark's Law represented a major achievement in economics in the 1940s. People at the time paid attention to structural issues. Prior to Clark, Fischer and co had done fruitful work on the classification of industries. They proposed the basic standards for industrial classification and formed a generally recognized theoretical paradigm. Economic development also manifested a certain correlation between industrial structure and economic growth. It is on this basis that Clark's Law was summarized and rose to prominence.

In his era, Clark's study was unduly rigorous. First of all, the conclusions he drew from the relationship between industrial structure and economic growth incorporated the latest findings and opened up an important field of analysis in the process and quality of economic growth. Secondly, Clark adopted a quantitative method to observe long-term economic growth. He examined changes of labor distribution among different industries in the growth process between the mid-19th century and mid-20th century, arriving at novel conclusions. Moreover, his multi-country comparison makes it clear that labor structure is more inclined to the tertiary industry in countries with higher per capita income. Clark's study was hailed as a law of economic development and supported by a group of authoritative scholars.

They pushed Clark's Law to the pinnacle of theory. Kuznets made up for the defect of Clark's Law in theoretical premise by presupposing "economic growth." Here, "economic growth" refers to the continuous increase of population in the long run rather than the short run, under the condition that per capita product does not decrease obviously or per capita product stabilizes or increases. In reality, "economic growth" is almost equivalent to time in the long run. Later, Chenery and Bell, who proposed the post-industrial society, again proved Clark's Law based on data extended to the 1970s. However, Clark's theory inevitably has implied limitations.

Firstly, Clark and his followers happened to focus on the later stage of industrial revolutions, when the industrial sector was in recession. They certainly helped in them concluding that the rise in service sector share is an inevitable development trend.

Secondly, in terms of research methods, Clark, Kuznets, Chenery, and Bell all compared the data of time nodes when the research periods started and ended. Though simple and clear, this approach ignored changes during these periods in the process of economic growth – when industrial revolution spurred industrial development and drove rapid economic growth. In fact, economic phenomena occur only at some points in the growth process.

Finally, new phenomena arising with the development of time creates room to doubt and deny traditional theories. Much of the material covered in earlier chapters, such as the Japanese debt-cycle crisis, Asian financial crisis, and US subprime mortgage crisis, occurred after the 1970s – i.e., after the research conducted by these scholars. I believe that if Clark and the others lived in the present, they would reflect on and reconstruct their analytical framework.

In short, we wish to emphasize that all theories have limitations. Such limitations are revealed by history. If a theory is regarded as an absolute truth, then it is no longer an interpretation of social activities, but more like a religion. This is true of Clark's Law and of other theories too. Only when practice contradicts its conclusions will we look into the defects of its theoretical premises and analytical methods. If we ignore the progress of time, these theories run the risk of becoming outdated.

II. *The Issue of Time*

New issues have arisen with the progression of time. As the prelude to the new industrial revolution opens, problems such as environmental and resource constraints, decline of traditional industry, overpopulation, labor shortages, and the Covid pandemic have arisen.

The first task is overcoming environmental and resource constraints. For centuries, humans have pursued economic development without factoring in these issues. However, faced with resource exhaustion and environmental deterioration, there have always been voices calling for the transformation of industrial structure and transition to a service-led economy. However, as aforementioned, the industrial sector is the dominant contributor to economic growth; the transition to a service-led economy will inevitably exhaust growth momentum. In the context of today's highly developed open economy, a certain region within a country or an economy with close international relations can form an economic bloc with other economies and leverage their industry to boost its services. As such, economic growth is relatively passive and economy lacks the material foundation to withstand the impact of economic crisis.

Even the US, which dominates global finance and prints the US dollar (the default global currency), could not overcome the drawbacks of long-term servitization. Given this, how can we achieve a positive situation in economic growth, environmental protection, and resource regeneration, simultaneously? It is actually easy: transform the technologies of traditional industry that harm the environment, instead using renewable resources in the production process. Environmental and resource problems accompanying industrial development are caused by industrial technology, rather than inherently by the industrial sector itself.

The second task is to find solutions for traditional industries. As industrial technology advances, traditional industries often face increased labor costs. In response, many companies have chosen to relocate: on an industrial scale, this process is described by Japanese economist Akamatsu as the "flying geese pattern." However, currently, the flying geese pattern has also been challenged. First, some traditional industries such as steel, coal and petrochemicals rely heavily on resources, and their transfer to resource-scarce areas is hindered to a certain extent by prospective increases in resource access costs. Second, even if costs can be reduced, environment damage discourages countries or regions from undertaking traditional industries. Especially today, when the concept of environmental protection has become deeply rooted, traditional industries may have nowhere to go if they do not revolutionize their technologies. Third, the new industrial revolution is in the ascendant, and technological innovations concerning new materials and energy are advancing rapidly. Traditional industry is vulnerable to complete elimination; without survival confidence, industrial transfer can be held off. Therefore, the flying geese pattern is only applicable to the middle stage of the long cycle between the two industrial revolutions, where industrial technology is mature and stable enough to support industrial transfer under labor cost pressures.

There are no more than two roads for traditional industries: i) Technological innovation – environment-friendly technologies can be adopted to support transformation of the new industrial system; ii) Industrial replacement enabled by technological innovation in new materials and energy. Traditional industries themselves will be completely withdrawn. In any case, these two roads must be premised on technological revolution. Industrial robots can be employed to replace labor, thereby solving cost issues. However, this fails to address environmental damage, and may even intensify damage due to efficiency improvement. In the end, traditional industries may linger, though industrial technological revolution is bound to occur.

The third task is coping with a diminishing demographic dividend. This has played an important role in China's economic growth, however some scholars have raised concerns about an aging population and proportional decrease in the workforce. This issue needs to be analyzed objectively and dialectically: the dependence on labor quantity and skills is inescapable whether for light industry (e.g. textiles and shoes), construction, or for traditional heavy industries. In the long run, however, there is no need to worry about such shortages. With the advancement of industrial technology, machinery will increasingly replace labor, bringing down the input of manpower. A processing factory that used to have thousands of workers will evolve into an unmanned factory in a very short period of time, with only a few program operators and mechanical maintenance technicians. While the real economy is being automated, the service sector is pushing for an unmanned automated business model. A typical example is unmanned supermarkets that have recently emerged. Hence, the anxiety about the disappearance of demographic dividend is actually derived from traditional industrial thinking, and is totally unnecessary. At present, more attention should be paid to the issue of income distribution associated with highly automated and unmanned industries. There are too few people engaged in production of the real economy that creates wealth. Correspondingly, the remuneration redistributed to the service sector is too limited to satisfy the demand for consumption that increases with the influx of the unemployed population. For this reason, institutional reform is also imperative.

Section 2   Direction of Industrial Development

Economic activities are always grounded in material production and carried out in accordance with the internal market mechanism. The service economy, meanwhile, is an accessory and derivative product of this. Practice has proved that pursuing the wrong industrial structure policy can only be challenged by reality in the process of specious exploration. A typical example is Clark's Law on the relationship between economic growth and industrial structure. The many painful lessons from economic virtualization and bubble development have not only prompted reflection on these theories, but also underlined the critical importance of developing the real economy. Currently, the subprime mortgage crisis, in essence, reflects the stagnation of the entire material production sector. Recognizing this, in order to shift the focus of economic activities to material production, the industrial system needs reshaping through industrial revolution.

I.   *Internal Mechanism of Industrial Revolution*

After the US subprime mortgage crisis broke out, countries generally came to realize the hazard of an over-developed service economy. In an active response, major nations have established their own industrial development strategies. Against the backdrop of severe financial crisis, a new round of industrial revolution has taken place and gained momentum.

In developed countries, the real economy often lacks vitality due to long-term technological stagnation. A large number of industries have been transferred to low-cost developing countries under various pressures such as rising labor costs, increasingly depleted resources, relative market shrinkage, diminishing profits etc. It is the abnormal development of services that drives domestic growth. This catalyzes the evolution of services, and fuels the excessive expansion of the virtual economy that ultimately leads to crisis. This is manifested in the recession of traditional industries, such as automobiles, steel, coal, and petrochemicals, after the outbreak of the crisis, represented by the bankruptcy of General Motors in the United States.

The new industrial revolution will not be a simple process of technological transformation of a few industries, but a comprehensive transformation of the existing system. It will address the lack of vitality in industrial development, and moreover, solve the long-standing fundamental problem that neglects the environment and resources.

Herein, the industrial technology system refers to a unified organic whole of various industrial technologies applied in different fields and intrinsically connected in the production process. Depending on the scope and degree of influence, these industrial technologies are divided into three technology levels: source, backbone, and branch. Source technology is the most influential – it determines the nature and essence of the entire industrial sector, and affects the generation, transformation, status and role of core technology in other industries. Backbone technology includes various industrial technologies inferior to, and directly in support of, source technology. It is not as influential as source technology in depth and breadth, and only has a major effect on one or a few industries. Branch technology covers the technologies used in specific production processes within each industry. It serves backbone technology in the system.

The survival crisis faced by the economy and society is associated, fundamentally, with the nature of the industrial system. Previous industrial revolutions have all neglected the relationship between man and nature in the development and application of industrial technologies. Consequently, industrial technologies at various levels entail the consumption of non-renewable resources and the discharge of waste pollution.

Evidence can be found through a brief review of the three industrial revolutions: The first represented by the steam engine in the 1860s marked a qualitative leap from agriculture to industry. The advent of the steam engine propelled the development of coal, metallurgy, machinery manufacturing, and transportation, opening the door to the rapid development and utilization of natural energy and materials by mankind. The second revolution was characterized by electric power and the internal combustion engine in the late 19th century, and increasing human plunder of non-renewable natural resources which added to environmental degradation. Industrial development was mainly powered by fossil energy. However, such dissipation of energy emitted various waste gases into the atmosphere and environment.

Clean water resources were reduced because various physical and chemical production processes employed clean water as a coolant or discharge carrier of poisonous and harmful substances. Vegetation also shrank sharply due to the exploitation of many mines. As cities expanded with population growth, factories and houses continued to encroach on limited arable land. The third revolution after WWII, represented by microelectronics, new materials, bioengineering, and aerospace, failed to change the intrinsic characteristics of large-scale industrial production. On the contrary, it has made such a technological system more sophisticated and advanced.

In short, the three industrial revolutions transformed the entire system by means of major changes in source technology. Although industrial productivity has improved, resource consumption and environmental pollution has not been alleviated. On this account, it is necessary to reform the current system for the purpose of sustainable development.

II. Policy Perspective of Industrial Revolution

At present, people still have a relatively narrow understanding of the new industrial revolution. The policies adopted by major economies largely aim to harness intelligent technology to improve traditional industries. In April 2009, former US President Barack Obama declared that the country would "reinvigorate the manufacturing industry." Subsequently, the US government successively published *A Strategy for American Innovation: Creating Quality Jobs and Lasting Economic Growth*, *The Manufacturing Enhancement Act of 2010*, and *A Strategy for American Innovation: Securing Our Economic Growth and Prosperity*. This highlighted advanced manufacturing, biotechnology, clean energy and other key areas. Furthermore, it launched other development plans. In early 2012, Germany unveiled its Industry 4.0 Strategy, focusing on the promotion of intelligent manufacturing. This has driven information technology development, renewable energy, new materials, and biological industries across Europe. Meanwhile, after the financial crisis in 2008, the Japanese government issued the Industrial Structure Vision 2010, identifying ten hi-tech industries such as the main strategic areas for future industrial development. In April 2016, the Ministry of Economy, Trade and Industry announced the New Industrial Structure Vision as a mid-term plan, pursuing economic growth spurred on by the latest technology.

In contrast, China began the strategy for industrial revolution, and proposed building a new industrial system. In March 2006, the Chinese Academy of Sciences published the *Mid- and Long-term Development Plan Outline*, predicting that new technological revolution will be unfolded in eight areas. These were information technology; life science and biotechnology; material science; material technology; resource and environmental technology; energy technology; space and ocean technology; and mathematics. Subsequently, the central government has successively promulgated documents on the promotion of the new industrial revolution. Among them are guidelines of national significance, such as the *Circular on Several Policies to Promote the Industrialization of Independent Innovation Achievements* (December 2008), *Circular on Further*

Supporting the Technological Innovation of Enterprises (November 2011), and *Thirteenth Five-Year Plan for National Development of Strategic Emerging Industries* (July 2012).

In May 2015, the State Council unveiled the Made in China 2025 strategy, which highlighted ten priority areas: 1) next generation information technology, 2) high-end automated machine tools and robots, 3) aerospace equipment, 4) marine equipment and high-tech shipping, 5) advanced rail transit equipment, 6) energy conservation and new energy vehicles, 7) power equipment, 8) agricultural machinery and equipment, 9) new materials, and 10) biomedicine and high-performance medical equipment. By clarifying the key areas and core tasks, this strategy has provided a programmatic guideline for the Chinese government to press on with the new industrial revolution. The release of the *Guiding Opinions on Accelerating Platform Construction for Mass Entrepreneurship and Innovation* (September 2015) underlines this.

In December 2015, the Chinese government further embarked on supply-side structural reforms. While enhancing the adaptability of supply structure to changes in demand, such reforms will increase total factor productivity, contributing to sustained and sound economic and social development. Five key tasks were laid down: reducing capacity, destocking, deleveraging, reducing costs, and making up for weak links. In short, among the world's major economies, only China has proposed building a new industrial system. Of course, other economies have not yet established such complete industrial systems.

III. Future Trends of Industry

To fundamentally change the established system, the new industrial revolution must start with the source technology of the Second Industrial Revolution, and cultivate new source technology according to the needs of actual social and economic development.

First, to meet sustainable development objectives, the new industrial revolution should address the conventional system that damages the environment and depletes natural resources. Current industrial technology is still dominated by heavy chemicals. The source technology underpinning this system, i.e., petroleum and the internal combustion engine, entails the consumption of non-renewable resources. These characteristics are then transmitted to backbone and branch technologies such as automobiles, steel, and metallurgy. Therefore, new energy and electric vehicles are deemed as pillars of the new industrial revolution.

Secondly, the new industrial revolution should alter the characteristics of mass production in response to individualized and diversified needs. To this end, it is necessary to take advantage of fast-developing network technology while employing intelligent manufacturing as source technology. A flexible production system should be developed, and with the help of intelligent machinery, a diversified production process can be enabled. Additionally, C2C, C2P and other information platforms should be set to keep abreast of market trends and carry out customized manufacturing. In most cases, this process does not transform backbone technology, but just makes intelligent changes to production, sales and management platforms.

In addition, the new industrial revolution should meet the needs of an aging society by lifting the human capital constraints on traditional production. Both the real economy and the service economy can develop robots to replace manpower, which can reduce costs and improve efficiency. For sure, intelligent manufacturing is more important and imperative for the industrial machinery industry, while there is an extremely urgent demand for machinery in the traditionally human-reliant agriculture.

Last but not least, the new industrial revolution must adapt to people's needs for physical and mental health, and comfortable lives. For this reason, the core areas will also cover the health industry, such as medicine and nursing. They will reshape the basic pattern of life – especially the basic pattern of healthcare consumption.

To sum up, the new industrial revolution is initiated to meet the overall needs of sustainable development and the individual needs of personalization, diversification, and convenience. It will fundamentally transform the technical system dominated by unsustainable heavy chemical industries; whilst it will also supplement and improve the existing system through the industrialization of new areas, such as intelligent technology and biotechnology. Now is the time to dispense with Clark's Law.

Index